SPACECRAFT VOYAGER 1
New and Selected Poems

SPACECRAFT VOYAGER 1

New and Selected Poems

❧ ❧

Alice Oswald

GRAYWOLF PRESS

Publication of this volume is made possible in part by a grant provided by the Minnesota State Arts Board, through an appropriation by the Minnesota State Legislature; a grant from the Wells Fargo Foundation Minnesota; and a grant from the National Endowment for the Arts, which believes that a great nation deserves great art. Significant support has also been provided by the Bush Foundation; Target; the McKnight Foundation; and other generous contributions from foundations, corporations, and individuals. To these organizations and individuals we offer our heartfelt thanks.

A Jane Kenyon book, funded in part by the Estate of Jane Kenyon to support the ongoing careers of women poets published by Graywolf Press.

NATIONAL
ENDOWMENT
FOR THE ARTS

MINNESOTA
STATE ARTS BOARD

TARGET.

Poems from *The Thing in the Gap-Stone Stile* were first published in Great Britain in 1996 by Oxford University Press.

Poems from *Dart* and *Woods etc.* were first published in Great Britain in 2002 and 2005 by Faber and Faber Limited, London.

Published by Graywolf Press
250 Third Avenue North, Suite 600
Minneapolis, Minnesota 55401
All rights reserved.

www.graywolfpress.org

Published in the United States of America

ISBN 978-1-55597-482-4

2 4 6 8 10 9 7 5 3

Library of Congress Control Number: 2007924771

Cover design: Christa Schoenbrodt, Studio Haus

Cover art: iStockphoto.com

Contents

SPACECRAFT VOYAGER 1
New and Selected Poems

FROM
The Thing in the Gap-Stone Stile

Pruning in Frost

Last night, without a sound,
a ghost of a world lay down on a world,

trees like dream-wrecks
coralled with increments of frost.

Found crevices
and wound and wound
the clock-spring cobwebs.

All life's ribbon frozen mid-fling.

Oh I am
stone thumbs,
feet of glass.

Work knocks in me the winter's nail.

I can imagine
Pain, turned heron,
could fly off slowly in a creak of wings.

And I'd be staring, like one of those
cold-holy and granite kings,
getting carved into this effigy of orchard.

A Greyhound in the Evening after a Long Day of Rain

Two black critical matching crows,
calling a ricochet, eating its answer,

dipped
    home

and a minute later
the ground was a wave and the sky wouldn't float.

    ≋ ≋

With a task and a rake,
with a clay-slow boot and a yellow mack,
I bolted for shelter under the black strake dripping of timber,

summer of rain, summer of green rain
coming everywhere all day down
though a hole in my foot.

    ≋ ≋

Listen Listen Listen Listen

    ≋ ≋

They are returning to the rain's den,
they grey folk, rolling up their veils,
taking the steel taps out of their tips and heels.

Grass lifts, hedge breathes,
rose shakes its hair,
birds bring out all their washed songs,
puddles like long knives flash on the roads.

    ≋ ≋

And evening is come with a late sun unloading a silence,
tiny begin-agains dancing on the night's edge.

But what I want to know is
whose is the great grey wicker-limber hound,
like a stepping on coal, going softly away . . .

The Glass House

The glass house is a hole in the rain,
the sun's chapel,
a bell for the wind.

Cucumbers, full of themselves,
the long green lungs of that still air,

image the fruits of staying put,
like water-beetles in woodland puddles
and hoofprints.

And I
am a hole in the glass house,
taking my time between the rows.

The leaves, the yellow blooms, the pots
vanish through a loop of thoughts.

Then far off
comes the cluck-sound of this green can
dipping and spilling . . .
and dipping again.

My Neighbour, Mrs Kersey

That noise, Mrs Kersey—were you listening?
A tin roof warping and booming . . .

Our sitting rooms connect like shears
into the screw-pin of our fires.

We share a bird's nest in a common chimney.
If I'm right, you breathe, Mrs Kersey,

close as a dream-self on the other side.
This wall, if you just rubbed an eyelid,

is a bricked-up looking glass.
And wind across that roof's a loss

of difference to whatever's moving
privately though our heads this evening.

Like the clicking of my jaw,
the tic-tac of your solitaire.

Poem

You ask me why did I lie down
and when and never rose again.

I of the bluebells
layed on a succulent mattress, frown.

And ask me when shall I get up
and blink and see my friends again.

I run my fingers round my lip,
transmuted to a bluebell cup.

A spider swings from bloom to bloom.
A fungus detonates and slowly
leaf contusions rot to rheum.

And every which way my fly-about eyes
catch this and that and my half-replies,
seduced by visions, vaporise.

It's when you've gone,
(the quiet woods creaking after rain),
my voice, a pollen dust, puffs out
the reason I remain:

here I give up the difficult dice
of friendship and I crook my knees
into a zed beneath the trees.
I watch in miniature of man
such intricate affairs as these,
these bluebells tussling for the sun.

since love is round and man misshapen
it may not always accord and if I
and I do furiously reprove myself
hackle up and without impulse cry
or if after if I hum for hours
all cold and odd and feign mad
and vanish with my jacket on my head
and your calm hands just lift and let it by . . .
I say a miracle a notion at risk
and grown of and aloof to faults and a
terrible demand is love but if you ask
something of refund on your gentleness
and in good time take secretly
another girl and say so guiltily . . .
then leave me I haven't such forgiveness . . .

April

The sheer grip and the push of it—growth gets
a footledge in the loosest stems, it takes
the litterings of weeds and clocks them round;
your eyeballs bud and alter and you can't
step twice in the same foot—I know a road,
the curve throws it one way and another;
somebody slipped the gears and bucketed slowly
into the hawthorns and his car took root
and in its bonnet now, amazing flowers
appear and fade and quiddify the month;
and us on bicycles—it was so fast
wheeling and turning we were lifted falling,
our blue-sky jackets filling up like vowels . . .
and now we float in the fair blow of springtime,
kingfishers, each astonishing the other
to be a feathered nerve, to take the crack
between the river's excess and the sun's.

Bike Ride on a Roman Road

This Roman road—eye's axis
over the earth's rococo curve—
is a road's road to ride in a dream.

I am bound to a star,
my own feet shoving me swiftly.

Everything turns but the North is the same.

Foot Foot, under the neck-high bracken
a little random man, with his head in a bad
controversy of midges,
flickers away singing Damn Damn

and the line he runs is serpentine,
everything happens at sixes and sevens,
the jump and the ditch and the crooked stile . . .

and my two eyes are floating in the fields,
my mouth is on a branch, my hair
is miles behind me making tributaries
and I have had my heart distracted out of me,
my skin is blowing slowly about without me

and now I have no hands and now I have no feet.

This is the road itself
riding a bone bicycle through my head.

Sea Sonnet

Green, grey and yellow, the sea and the weather
instantiate each other and the spectrum
turns in it like a perishable creature.
The sea is old but the blue sea is sudden.

The wind japans the surface. Like a flower,
each point of contact biggens and is gone.
And when it rains the senses fold in four.
No sky, no sea—the whiteness is all one.

So I have made a little moon-like hole
with a thumbnail and through a blade of grass
I watch the weather make the sea my soul,
which is a space performed on by a space;

and when it rains, the very integer
and shape of water disappears in water.

Sea Sonnet

The sea is made of ponds—a cairn of rain.
It has an island flirting up and down
like a blue hat. A boat goes in between.

Is made of rills and springs—each waternode
a tiny subjectivity, the tide
coordinates their ends, the sea is made.

The sea crosses the sea, the sea has hooves;
the powers of rivers and the weir's curves
are moving in the wind-bent acts of waves.

And then the softer waters of the wells
and soakaways—hypostases of holes,
which swallow up and sink for seven miles;

and then the boat arriving on the island
and nothing but the sea-like sea beyond.

Sea Sonnet

A field, a sea-flower, three stones, a stile.
Not one thing close to another
throughout the air. The cliff's uplifted lawns.
You and I walk light as wicker in virtual contact.

Prepositions lie exposed. All along
the swimmer is deeper than the water.
I have looked under the wave,
I saw your body floating on the darkness.

Oh time and water cannot touch.
Not touch. Only a blob far out,
your singularity and the sea's
inalienable currents flow at angles . . .

and if I love you this is incidental
as on the sand one blue towel, one white towel.

Estuary Sonnet

As much as I walk by and see the water
up to the second line, I skim a slate
and in the time it sinks my feet are wet
and there are huge boats lifting in the harbour.

And then as far as I have time to wander,
I wander back and there's a heron's foot
lofting the water which is now a mud-flat
and some old shipwreck gnawn to its vertebrae.

Touch me the moment where these worlds collide,
the river's cord unravelled by the tide . . .

and I will show you nothing—neither high
nor low nor salt nor fresh—only the skill
of tiny creatures like the human eye
to live by water, which is never still.

Ballad of a Shadow

Take from me my voice and I shall voiceless go
to find you; take from me my face,
I'll trek the hills invisibly,
·my strength, and I shall run but keep no pace.

Even in cities, take the sense with which I reason
and I shall seek, but close it in your heart,
keep this and forget this
and this, when we're apart,

will be the shadow game of love.
And I shall love in secret
and I shall love in crowds
and love in darkness, in the quiet

outlet of shadows, and in cities
as a ghost walking unnoticed,
and love with books, using their pages like a wind,
not reading, and with people, latticed

by words but through the lattice loving.
And when at last my love is understood,
with you I shall not love but breathe
and turn by breathing into flesh and blood.

Wedding

From time to time our love is like a sail
and when the sail begins to alternate
from tack to tack, it's like a swallowtail
and when the swallow flies it's like a coat;
and if the coat is yours, it has a tear
like a wide mouth and when the mouth begins
to draw the wind, it's like a trumpeter
and when the trumpet blows, it blows like millions . . .
and this, my love, when millions come and go
beyond the need of us, is like a trick;
and when the trick begins, it's like a toe
tip-toeing on a rope, which is like luck;
and when the luck begins, it's like a wedding,
which is like love, which is like everything.

If Stones Could Fly

Having watched a spider closely,
I find there is a stone in it,
cleverly lifted and set rolling,
like a kite manoeuvres a man.

Or an orbit, approaching its pole
by compensatory poise and pull,
corybantic and following threads
and doing shrift of spooling and crawling,

visions of unspannable air
spin her, making the silk a wheel
that struts and hubs and rims a gap
between a rafter and a sack.

But it's a stone's life—this needing a web—
and what'd fly if it were made
is tethered to a dropping thing
which halves the loveliness of floating.

The Thing in the Gap-Stone Stile

I took the giant's walk on top of world,
peak-striding, each step a viaduct.

I dropped hankies, cut from a cloth of hills,
and beat gold under fields
for the sun to pick out a patch.

I never absolutely told
the curl-horned cows to line up their gaze.
But it happened, so I let it be.

And Annual Meadow Grass, quite of her own accord,
between the dry-stone spread out emerald.

(I was delighted by her initiative
and praised the dry-stone for being contrary.)

What I did do (I am a gap)
was lean these elbows on a wall
and sat on my hunkers pervading the boulders.

My pose became the pass across two kingdoms,
before behind antiphonal, my cavity the chord.

And I certainly intended
anyone to be almost
abstracted on a gap-stone between fields.

Mountains

Something is in the line and air along edges,
which is in woods when the leaf changes
and in the leaf-pattern's gives and gauges,
the water's tension upon ledges.
Something is taken up with entrances,
which turns the issue under bridges.
The moon is between places.
An outlet fills the space between two horses.

Look through a holey stone. Now put it down.
Something is twice as different. Something gone
accumulates a queerness. Be alone.
Something is side by side with anyone.

And certain evenings, something in the balance
falls to the dewpoint where our minds condense
and then inslides itself between moments
and spills the heart from its circumference;
and this is when the moon matchlessly opens
and you can feel by instinct in the distance
the bigger mountains hidden by the mountains,
like intentions among suggestions.

The Melon Grower

She concerned him,
but the connection had come loose.
They made shift with tiffs and silence.

He sowed a melon seed.
He whistled in the greenhouse.
She threw a slipper at him

and something jostled in the loam
as if himself had been layed blind.
She misperceived him. It rained.

The melon got eight leaves, it lolled.
She banged the plates.
He considered his fretful webby hands.

'If I can sex' he said 'the flowers,
very gently I'll touch their parts
with a pollen brush made of rabbit hairs.'

The carpels swelled. He had to prop them on pots.
She wanted the house repainting.
He was out the back watering.

He went to church, he sang 'O Lord how long shall the wicked . . . ?'
He prayed, with his thumbs on his eyes.
His head, like a melon, pressured his fingers.

The shoots lengthened
and summer mornings came with giant shadows
and arcs as in the interim of a resurrection.

She stayed in bed, she was coughing.
He led the side-shoots along the wires.
She threw the entire tea-trolley downstairs.

And when the milk was off
and when his car had two flat tyres
and when his daughter left saying she'd had enough,

he was up a ladder hanging soft nets from the beam
to stop the fruit so labouring the stem.
The four globes grew big at ease

and a melony smell filled the whole place
and he caught her once, confused in the greenhouse,
looking for binder-twine. Or so she says.

Prayer

Here I work in the hollow of God's hand
with Time bent round into my reach. I touch
the circle of the earth, I throw and catch
the sun and moon by turns into my mind.
I sense the length of it from end to end,
I sway me gently in my flesh and each
point of the process changes as I watch;
the flowers come, the rain follows the wind.

And all I ask is this—and you can see
how far the soul, when it goes under flesh,
is not a soul, is small and creaturish—
that every day the sun comes silently
to set my hands to work and that the moon
turns and returns to meet me when it's done.

The Three Wise Men of Gotham
Who Set Out to Catch the Moon
in a Net

Introduction

In the thirteenth century, the people of Gotham were expecting a visit from King John. This would have been expensive (it involved collection of taxes and even the laying of a road to welcome him), so they decided to put him off by pretending to be mad. They began drowning eels, fishing for the moon, getting dressed by jumping out of trees into trousers; they even built a wall around a thicket to stop a cuckoo escaping. This, they said, would prolong the spring. King John avoided the town.

This poem describes their journey to catch the moon. It includes a reference to Thomas Love Peacock's song:

Seamen three! What men be ye?
Gotham's three wise men we be . . .
Who art thou, so fast adrift?
I am he they call Old Care . . .

and also to the legend of seven fishermen who came home in tears because one of their company had drowned; in fact they had simply miscalculated: each man was counting the six people he could see, and forgetting himself.

It was a monday night. The moon was up
and throwing golden elvers on the water.
Long bows of wind were swerving on the quay.
A man came down, whose purpose was to catch
the watermoon—whatever flower or fish
the light took shape as, shifting and dividing.
He was a butcher. He came shouting by
as if the art of thinking were a pommel
to pound the world into conformity;
'The moon,' he said, 'in that it is a magnet,
moves independently and has a soul,
the motor principle of which . . .' the wind
had found a cave of whispers in his coat
and in a line of sailing boats a tune
to jingle on the halyards; tiny waves
were running in the puddles . . . 'O the moon—
how many miles' he said 'to catch a moon?'

He had two friends—a baker and a maker
of candlesticks—who didn't know the answer.
The one had been on nights, laying the loaves
in rows in stainless trays, when he looked up
and saw this woman floating in the window:
'Ave Maria the moon is full of grace . . .'
He dropped his knife. He switched the ovens off
and ran to meet the butcher in the harbour
just as the other, in his dark workshop
where he was turning woodblocks into spirals
to make a candlestick, the loveliness
and quiet of moonlight drew him to the door;
and he was blind—a single iron wire
ran through his eyelids, stitching them together—
but even so, the moon enchanted him
to move by touch and spaces to the harbour.

'Who's there?' 'Who's with you?' 'No one' 'just the moon'
'Can I come with you?' 'I was half asleep'

'What IS that noise?' 'and I could hear this form
breathing at the back door—I mean the sea'
'the sea's the sea' 'throw me the net' 'what's that?'
'That's holes in it to keep it light' 'shhhh'
Three cut-out shadows moving on a wall,
a rowing boat pushed like a wooden slipper
over a shelf of shingle . . . two foot down,
it came alive and lifted in the waves.

'Hold steady now!' The two men jumped aboard.
The third, the baker, was knee-deep in water
shoving them slowly out. He felt the hoops
of ice-cold sea contracting on his thighs
and far and wide around him he could hear,
in all that toil of suction and secretion,
the bird-like stones calling under the breakers;
the pied stones and the grey and pigeon stones
and black and round and rolling and knocking
white-throated stones that warble in the wash.
'The sea is full' he said, 'not just of fish
but I can hear the winged souls of the drowned
transforming into pebbles' 'shh—no more.'
'Get in the boat, whip to it, coil the cable;
Candle, you take the oars. As you're a turner
you'll understand these wooden pruned up things.
I'll guide us out. Head for the fishing boats.
There are some dark ones lying big at ease
in the middle water, swinging their prows
as if they grazed their shadows in their sleep.
We want to steer as near them as we dare
to slide above the sandbar to the sea.'

So Candle sculls them slowly from the shallows,
the sea on runners, letting it give and hold
as if his hands are at a factory loom
of miles of silk and moving cylinders;

and he stares up into the stone of his eyes,
he lifts the oars, he feels a bigger darkness,
he yields and feels, controls and strokes and hollows,
carving a sea-form with his arms—a sphere,
a curvilinear figure with two holes.
He rows them out over the long reflections
of window-lights. They go beyond the boatyard,
where metals clank all night. It bangs and dings
as they go rocking for the open sea.

Now he has hitched his heartbeat to the oars.
He rows by breathing, like a mower mows
dreaming a lawn though thirty parallels;
and as they pass the fishing boats, the wind
freshens and blows a circle on their necks
and everywhere the trees, all down the cliffs
are running to them in a shape of waving
like haiku trees, staggering to keep up
the impetus of an extended instant,
and they can hear semi-attentively
the after-differences of sound on sea—
the boom of aeroplanes as they go low
rumbling a bay-wide echo endlessly
and the cuneiform cries of the sea birds
and human voices stopping in mid-air
and under every sound, the lines of water:
'Nunc dimittis Domine' they whisper,
'swish' they whisper 'flutter the boat with wind,
wash it away according to thy word . . .'

'Everything moves' says Candle, 'even Gotham,
even the harbour wall is slowly moving
and if I dip my oar-blade and my oar-blade
there grows another wave between each splash.
How can I row a line consistently
when I can't see, unless I row by spells—

no shape, no place—it is the mastery
of one dark soul over another soul,
this movement of three men over the water.'

The sea is high. They have climbed a black wave
into another world of three steps long
and overboard and only one step wide.
On either side of them a curve. They pause.
They feel it like a tremor in a window
flicker across itself and drop away
and then they slide into the roller vallies
and wavetops crash on them like rotten trees.
The baker bails, the candlemaker rows,
the butcher almost pukes to have the sea
spinning beneath him into scimitars:
the hissing noises as it cuts and meets
and murmurs and the world goes flat again;
and then the thousand epileptic patterns,
the flowers, the momentary islamic marks
which the wind makes on water, all the flash
and twirl and slap and rivalry of waves
mount into aspects of a nothingness
which strives to hold, to make itself by moving.

And then that other sea—the sky. Dark clouds,
the images of waves, were breaking,
falling towards their water-selves as rain;
and in the thick of it, the moon
opened a golden eyelid and looked down,
looked once, looked twice and closed. 'There is no moon.
The moon's gone out' said Butcher, 'this is rain.'
'They say,' said Baker, 'if you oil the moon,
the night goes twice as fast as if you don't.'

The waves that night were everything by turns.
Sometimes they had to shout above the blows
to make themselves be heard and sometimes whispers

competed with the footfall of the oars
and they were rowing in a quiet cathedral.
But it was deafman's buff. The three old men,
they felt as if some power had entered them
and turned their words to foam, they couldn't care
how much they heard, they answered all at once . . .

'What is the moon?' said Candle. 'Is it round?
Do you imagine it an appliqué,
flat like a leaf of gold? Is it so high?'
'The moon is made of water' 'sea is water'
'Somehow the water isn't yet the sea—
it is wave on wave a body struggling
under construction to be something else'
'and the full moon is held in the sea's mind
as her spiritual end' 'the moon is light'
'the sea is light' 'the sea seeks to be round
as if her tides could make a moon by rolling'
'mare imbrium' 'mare nubium'
'mare humorum' 'sinus irridum'
'what unifies the sea?' 'the sea's conjunctions'
'it has it sideways up then flat then sideways'
'the sea contains two spirits lifting glass
who pass each other watching the sharp edge'
'it's a controversy!' 'we sound like waves'
'we sound as if the wind has blown us high
and we must roar until we crumble' 'shhh . . .'

The sea had mastered them. They couldn't make
even the simplest sense of what they witnessed:
the moon, the birds, the crooked boat. They moved
far out between absurdity and wonder,
rocking like figures in a nursery rhyme,
the waves like great smooth beasts shoving them on.

How many men? How many miles from Gotham?
How many fish, feet, hands? They couldn't count.

They only knew the waves were twice as high
and twice as endless as they wished and each
stroke of the oar, each splash, the green-souled waves
came cold alive with pricks of phosphorus
and whispered messages of random numbers:
'Three men, three men of Gotham in a bowl,
the man of Gotham in the moon, the sea,
the six or seven common brittle stars,
and one was blind and two was terrified,
meganyctophanes, four men of Gotham
was hard to balance in the bowl, the moon,
it wasn't even safe to raise a finger
to make a tally of the crew but always
three men three men of Gotham in the moan,
the velvet swimming crab, the file, the flatworm . . .'

And this is why such arguments arose
as to the numbers. They were so confused—
it was like standing in an ancient circle
counting the broken stones, or in a dream
counting your hands and finding three—or four—
that as it happened, each of them in turn
counted the others and forgot himself:
'that's one, that's two of us—so where's the third?'
'I can't see anything' 'has someone gone?'
'listen, who's missing' 'do it with your eyes,
in ones and starting with the first' 'one two'
'halibu crackibu' 'and who's to say
whether or not the laws of quantities
apply at sea where everything is moving?'
'things disappear' 'the minute we relax
the waves have washed them from the boat' 'and now?'
'I don't know who's not here, but let the rower
starboard about and head for home in silence.'

No one did anything. The candlemaker
was too afraid to turn. He kept on rowing

and muttering the music of the oars:
'You say there's two of us. You say I'm blind.
I'm frightened. There's no end to where we are.
People have sunk here. It isn't water,
it's fear of light, the proof of sea is fear.
And I can see myself caught in this fear,
rowing a boat of ghosts—you see I can see—
I can see four of us, I heard a man
beating the flocks of horrid barking waves
towards this boat and now he's in with us . . .
there I can feel us: one and two and three
and four of us—we've got an extra man . . .'

Imagine this cold moment: here's the butcher
trying to wipe the error from his eyes;
and here's the baker, counting on his fingers,
his tongue thick, his lips like fluttering eyelids;
the candlemaker with his chin uptilted
tracing a circle in the air; the wind
dead as a doornail. And the fourth person,
now dim, now clear—all they can see of him
is something breathing in the bows, the waves
shaking their wings like summoners behind him—
he makes a movement in the dark, the tshh
of someone moving forward in wet clothes.
The balance alters in the boat. He says:

'I am Old Care   it is my freezing round
to work these seas   many miles out and in
I walk swim fly   half like an oystercatcher
the shaky water under me   always
my feet wet, the ridges blue on my hands
I must make shift even in snow   the cliffs
the webs and cloths of frozen waterfalls
after the cold month when I have fallen
headlong frozen in mid-air   they give way
and spring comes the seathrift comes the gorse comes

the summer birds the sickle path of shoals
comes up the coast and little fishing boats
move out and out for mackerel bright as knives
this is my task   I have to turn seafarers
to water by despair   I call to them
with a mad bird cry   nami no tsuzumi
look at the endlessness   the sea yellow
a level fetch of low saltwater waves
wears them away and it is I—Old Care
sits on the boatside silent without meaning.
I take hope out   I lift the very pearl
out of the dark eye-pupil while it's looking
on waves and waterpatterns   and I dive
I half take off I leave him suddenly
whoever I go haunting   staring down
a metre from the edge   and this is all
only the weather like a painted ball
thrown round and round and round him till he dies'

There were three men of Gotham in a boat,
almost in tears, without a thing to think
but shhh and that was endless, staring down
a metre from the edge of mind. The wind
had blown them wide with nothing to defend
except a little wavy line of seagulls,
tucked in the leeside of the gunwhales, drifting
and paddling back, with feathers soft and lifting.
'What reason do we' shhh—there was this boat
which held them like a rotten half potato;
they could have rolled it over on its side
and swum for heaven, but they sat as tight
as if they'd anchored on the interface
between two wastelands—life and fear of life.

The moon appeared, washed lovelier by rain.
The men three-quarters turned, they quarter-turned,
they tipped their faces broadside to the moon.

The moon appeared and disappeared, appeared
and disappeared and then appeared appeared.
The boat was light with reference to the moon
as if the two connected, but each one
was moving half in touch and half in shadow
and every face was different and alone;
and in the spin of moonshine, there were clouds
flying in zones like zodiacal creatures,
but without pace because the wind had gone.
The sea was miles and miles of palish tin
and a small countermoon was floating there,
very clear, very irregular perfect—
an aspirin in the middle of the world

and may the mystery move them now—the sea
cannot be finished with; each layer is layed
co-terminous with light but more than light
and seamless and invisible in water—
cannot be closed or opened, only entered . . .

'Don't speak' said Butcher, 'quickly, steer us round
the weather side, until your hair blows forward,
then quiet the boat.' The baker took an oar,
the candlemaker shuffled to the bows,
the butcher hugged the net and hoiked it out
in corkscrews from the hold. It was quite wet.
He draped it on the thwarts. The baker slewed
a figure of an eight with the spare oar,
which brought them to the luff side of the moon.
'O moon' said Candle, 'be extraordinary'
'be caught' said Butcher, 'prove that we were wise
to come so far—please—save us from the sea.'
'Amen' said Baker and they threw the net.
They steered away, they pulled the running cord,
the net turned over like a purse, it rose
into the moon and through the moon and out;
the moon broke up in pieces and came whole.

Three times they cast the driftnet, drew it up
and saw the moon dismantle, saw the net
grope for a ghost and gather what it could
and ropes of water reeve themselves away.
Three times the moon was shattered like a bowl
and slowly mended by the moon.

                       The moon
was in another world, the moon was flying
amazed around a floating point, the sea
was upside down in air and touching nothing
and without purpose there was fluke and balance
of light on water moving across water,
which broke in pieces and came whole again.

'Is it alive?' said Candle, 'Can I feel?
Have you gone quiet with the weight of it
or cold or what? Or is it what I thought—
that we're the prisoners—that the moon herself
has caught us in a net; if we step out
over the border of our wooden bowl,
I know what world there is, what huge sea-light
blinds us, winds like a chain through everything . . .'

No sound, only the knocking of the boatwood,
the net clacking its floats; until the darkness,
in living moments like a bud, gives way
to paler clouds, the almost apple green
and ice blue lines increase above the sea
and squares of water, pink and pea-leaf green
catch fire as if the sea became a star;
and after that, as I came down through Gotham,
that light which the horizons of all seas
imply beyond—a kind of agitated
surreal and weightless curve—I saw it move
to close the space above a tiny boat
and in that boat, I thought I saw three men

and one was standing like a cormorant
who dries his wings; the spinning of the earth,
the wind, the sun were pulling them away.
I heard their voices on the waves: 'Look up'
'what's that?' 'it's water' 'it's the moon' 'how far?'
'how many miles is it?' 'if we go on
beyond the crack of the horizon, wind
has broken down the moon. Silver in handfuls
and leaf of gold are floating on the sea'
'how shall we carry it?' 'we've got a bowl,
but it's a sea that may go on some time—
give me the left oar, Baker—close your eyes
and when the journey ends, I'll give a shout.'

Dart

'water always comes with an ego and an alter ego'

IVAN ILLYICH

This poem is made from the language of people who live and work on the Dart. Over the past two years I've been recording conversations with people who know the river. I've used these records as life-models from which to sketch out a series of characters—linking their voices into a sound-map of the river, a songline from the source to the sea. There are indications in the margin where one voice changes into another. These do not refer to real people or even fixed fictions. All voices should be read as the river's mutterings.

A.O.

Who's this moving alive over the moor?

An old man seeking and finding a difficulty.

Has he remembered his compass his spare socks
does he fully intend going in over his knees off the
    military track from Okehampton?

keeping his course through the swamp spaces
and pulling the distance around his shoulders

the source of the Dart
—Cranmere Pool on
Dartmoor, seven
miles from the nearest
road

and if it rains, if it thunders suddenly
where will he shelter looking round
and all that lies to hand is his own bones?

tussocks, minute flies,
        wind, wings, roots

He consults his map. A huge rain-coloured wilderness.
This must be the stones, the sudden movement,
the sound of frogs singing in the new year.
Who's this issuing from the earth?

The Dart, lying low in darkness calls out Who is it?
trying to summon itself by speaking . . .

the walker replies

An old man, fifty years a mountaineer, until my heart gave out,
so now I've taken to the moors. I've done all the walks, the Two
Moors Way, the Tors, this long winding line the Dart

this secret buried in reeds at the beginning of sound I
won't let go of man, under
his soakaway ears and his eye ledges working
into the drift of his thinking, wanting his heart

I keep you folded in my mack pocket and I've marked in red
where the peat passes are and the good sheep tracks

cow-bones, tin-stones, turf-cuts.
listen to the horrible keep-time of a man walking,
rustling and jingling his keys
at the centre of his own noise,
clomping the silence in pieces and I

I don't know, all I know is walking. Get dropped off the military track
from Oakenhampton and head down into Cranmere pool. It's dawn,
it's a huge sphagnum kind of wilderness, and an hour in the morning
is worth three in the evening. You can hear plovers whistling, your
feet sink right in, it's like walking on the bottom of a lake.

What I love is one foot in front of another. South-south-west and down
the contours. I go slipping between Black Ridge and White Horse Hill
into a bowl of the moor where echoes can't get out

listen,
a
lark
spinning
around
one
note
splitting
and
mending
it

and I find you in the reeds, a trickle coming out of a bank, a foal of
a river

one step-width water
of linked stones
trills in the stones
glides in the trills
eels in the glides
in each eel a fingerwidth of sea

in walking boots, with twenty pounds on my back: spare socks, compass, map, water purifier so I can drink from streams, seeing the cold floating spread out above the morning,

tent, torch, chocolate, not much else.

Which'll make it longish, almost unbearable between my evening meal and sleeping, when I've got as far as stopping, sitting in the tent door with no book, no saucepan, not so much as a stick to support the loneliness

he sits clasping his knees, holding his face low down between them,
he watches black slugs,
he makes a little den of his smells and small thoughts
he thinks up a figure far away on the tors
waving, so if something does happen,
if night comes down and he has to leave the path
then we've seen each other, somebody knows where we are.

falling back on appropriate words

turning the loneliness in all directions . . .

through Broadmarsh,   under Cut Hill,

Sandyhole, Sittaford, Hartyland, Postbridge,

Belever, Newtake, Dartmeet, the whole
unfolding emptiness branching and reaching
and bending over itself.

I met a man sevenish by the river
where it widens under the main road
and adds a strand strong enough
to break branches and bend back necks.

Rain. Not much of a morning.
Routine work, getting the buckets out
and walking up the cows—I know you,
Jan Coo. A wind on a deep pool.

Cows know him, looking for the fork in the dark.
They know the truth of him—a strange man—
I'm soaked, fuck these numb hands.
A tremor in the woods. A salmon under a stone.

I know who I am, I
come from the little heap of stones up by Postbridge,
you'll have seen me feeding the stock, you can tell it's me
because of the wearing action of water on bone.

Oh I'm slow and sick, I'm
trying to talk myself round to leaving this place,
but there's roots growing round my mouth, my foot's
in a rusted tin. One night I will.

And so one night he sneaks away downriver,
told us he could hear voices woooo
we know what voices means, Jan Coo Jan Coo.
A white feather on the water keeping dry.

Next morning it came home to us he was drowned.
He should never have swum on his own.
Now he's so thin you can see the light
through his skin, you can see the filth in his midriff.

Now he's the groom of the Dart—I've seen him
taking the shape of the sky, a bird, a blade,
a fallen leaf, a stone—may he lie long
in the inexplicable knot of the river's body

in a place of bracken and scattered stone piles and cream teas in the tourist season, comes the chambermaid unlocking every morning with her peach-soap hands: Only me, Room-Cleaning, number twenty-seven, an old couple—he's blind, she's in her nineties. They come every month walking very slowly to the waterfall. She guides him, he props her. She sees it, he hears it. Gently resenting each other's slowness: (Where are we turning you are tending to slide is it mud what is that long word meaning burthensome it's as if mud was issuing from ourselves don't step on the trefoil listen a lark going up in the dark would you sshhhhh?) Brush them away, squirt everything, bleach and vac and rubberglove them into a bin-bag, please do not leave toenails under the rugs, a single grey strand in the basin

shhh I can make myself invisible   Naturalist
with binoculars in moist places. I can see frogs
hiding under spawn—water's sperm—whisper, I wear soft colours

whisper, this is the naturalist
she's been out since dawn
dripping in her waterproof notebook

I'm hiding in red-brown grass all different lengths, bog bean, sundew, I get excited by its wetness, I watch spiders watching aphids, I keep my eyes in crevices, I know two secret places, call them x and y where the Large Blue Butterflies are breeding, it's lovely, the male chasing the female, frogs singing lovesongs

she loves songs, she belongs to the soundmarks of larks

I knew a heron once, when it got up
its wings were the width of the river,
I saw it eat an eel alive
and the eel the eel chewed its way back inside out through the heron's
    stomach

like when I creep through bridges right in along a ledge to see where the
    dippers nest.
Going through holes, I love that, the last thing through here was an otter

(two places I've seen eels, bright whips of flow   by the bridge, an eel
like stopper waves the rivercurve slides through   watcher
trampling around at first you just make out
the elver movement of the running sunlight
three foot under the road-judder you hold
and breathe contracted to an eye-quiet world
while an old dandelion unpicks her shawl
and one by one the small spent oak flowers fall
then gently lift a branch brown tag and fur
on every stone and straw and drifting burr
when like a streamer from your own eye's iris
a kingfisher spurts through the bridge whose axis
is endlessly in motion as each wave
photos its flowing to the bridge's curve
if you can keep your foothold, snooping down
then suddenly two eels let go get thrown
tumbling away downstream looping and linking
another time we scooped a net through sinking
silt and gold and caught one strong as bike-chain
stared for a while then let it back again
I never pass that place and not make time
to see if there's an eel come up the stream
I let time go as slow as moss, I stand
and try to get the dragonflies to land
their gypsy-coloured engines on my hand)

whose voice is this who's talking in my larynx
who's in my privacy under my stone tent
where I live slippershod in my indoor colours
who's talking in my lights-out where I pull to
under the bent body of an echo are these your
fingers in my roof are these your splashes

Everyone converges on bridges, bank holidays it fills up with cars, people set up tables in the reeds, but a mile either side you're back into wilderness. (*Twelve horses clattering away.*) and there's the dipper bobbing up and down like a man getting ready, hitching his trousers. I'm crouching, I never let my reflection fall on water,

I depend on being not noticed, which keeps me small and rather nimble, I can swim miles naked with midges round my head, watching wagtails, I'm soft, I'm an otter streaking from the headwaters, I run overland at night, I watch badgers, I trespass, don't say anything, I've seen waternymphs, I've seen tiny creatures flying, trapped, inter-marrying, invisible

upriver creatures born into this struggle against
water out of balance being swept away
mouthparts clinging to mosses

round streamlined creatures born into vanishing
between golden hide-outs, trout at the mercy of rush
quiver to keep still always

swimming up through it hiding
freshwater shrimps driven flat in this struggle against
haste pitching through stones

things suck themselves to rocks
things swinging from side to side
leak out a safety line to a leaf and

grip for dear life a sandgrain or gravel for ballast
thrown into this agony of being swept away
with ringing everywhere though everything is also silent

the spider of the rapids running over the repeated note
of disorder and rhythm in collision, the simulacrum fly
spinning a shelter of silk among the stones

and all the bright-feathered flies of the fishermen, indignant under the waterfall, in waders, getting their feet into position to lean over and move the world: medics, milkmen, policemen, millionaires, cheering themselves up with the ratchet and swish of their lines

fisherman and bailiff

I've payed fifty pounds to fish here and I fish like hell, I know the etiquette—who wades where—and I know the dark places under stones where things are moving. I caught one thirteen pounds at Belever, huge, silvery, maybe seven times back from the sea, now the sea-trout, he's canny, he'll keep to his lie till you've gone, you have to catch him at night.

Which is where the law comes in, the bailiff, as others see me, as I see myself when I wake, finding myself in this six-foot fourteen-stone of flesh with letters after my name, in boots, in a company vehicle, patrolling from the headwaters to the weir, with all my qualified faculties on these fish.

When the owls are out up at Newtake. You cast behind and then forwards in two actions. Casting into darkness for this huge, it's like the sea's right there underneath you, this invisible

now I know my way round darkness, I've got night vision, I've been up here in the small hours waiting for someone to cosh me but

it's not frightening if you know what you're doing. There's a sandbar, you can walk on it right across the weirpool but

I hooked an arm once, petrified, slowly pulling a body up, it was only a cardigan

but when you're onto a salmon,
a big one hiding under a rock, you can see his tail making the water
    move,
you let the current work your fly

all the way from Iceland, from the Faroes,
a three-sea-winter fish coming up on the spate,
on the full moon, when the river spreads out

a thousand feet between Holne and Dartmeet and he climbs it,
up the trickiest line, maybe
maybe down-flowing water has an upcurrent nobody knows

it takes your breath away,
generations of them inscribed into this river,
up at Belever where the water's only so wide

you can see them crowded in there
shining like tin, the hen-fish swishing her tail
making a little vortex, lifting the gravel

which is where the law comes in—I know all the articles, I hide in
the bushes with my diploma and along comes the Tavistock boys,
they've only got to wet their arms and grab, it's like shoplifting.
Names I won't mention. In broad daylight, in the holding pools. Run
up and stone the water and the salmon dodges under a ledge. Copper
snares, three-pronged forks—I know what goes on, I'm upfront but
I'm tactful.

I wear green for the sake of kingfishers.

I walk across the weir, on the phone in the middle of the river,
technically effective, at ease in my own power,
working my way downstream doing rod-license checks

with his torch, taking his own little circle of light
through pole-straight pinewoods,
slippy oakwoods, sudden insurrections of rowan,
reedholes and poor sour fields,
in the thick of bracken, keeping the law
from dwindling away

through Belever Whiteslade

Babeny

Newtake

(meanwhile the West Dart pours through   the West Dart rises
Crow Tor Fox Holes   under Cut Hill, not
Longaford Beardown and Wystman's Wood   .   far from the source of
and under Crockern Tor, singing   the East Dart

where's Ernie? Under the ground   the dead tinners speak

where's Redver's Webb? Likewise.

Tom, John and Solomon Warne, Dick Jorey, Lewis Evely?

Some are photos, others dust.
Heading East to West along the tin lodes,
80 foot under Hexworthy, each with a tallow candle in his hat.

Till rain gets into the stone,
which washes them down to the valley bottoms
and iron, lead, zinc, copper, calcite
and gold, a few flakes of it
getting pounded between the pebbles in the river.

Bert White, John Coaker.
Frank Hellier, Frank Rensfield,
William Withycombe, Alex Shawe, John Dawe, William
    Friend,
their strength dismantled and holding only names

Two Bridges, Dunnabridge, Hexworthy)

Dartmeet—a mob of waters
where East Dart smashes into West Dart

two wills gnarling and recoiling
and finally knuckling into balance

in that brawl of mudwaves
the East Dart speaks Whiteslade and Babeny

the West Dart speaks a wonderful dark fall
from Cut Hill through Wystman's Wood

put your ear to it, you can hear water
cooped up in moss and moving

slowly uphill through lean-to trees
where every day the sun gets twisted and shut

with the weak sound of the wind
rubbing one indolent twig upon another

and the West Dart speaks roots in a pinch of clitters
the East Dart speaks coppice and standards

the East Dart speaks the Gawler Brook and the Wallabrook
the West Dart speaks the Blackabrook that runs by the prison

at loggerheads, lying next to one another on the riverbed
wrangling away into this valley of oaks

forester

and here I am coop-felling in the valley, felling small sections to give
the forest some structure. When the chainsaw cuts out the place
starts up again. It's Spring, you can work in a wood and feel the earth
turning

woodman working on your own   waternymph
knocking the long shadows down
and all day the river's eyes
peep and pry among the trees

when the lithe water turns
and its tongue flatters the ferns
do you speak this kind of sound:
whirlpool whisking round?

Dart is old Devonian
for oak

Listen, I can clap and slide
my hollow hands along my side.
Imagine the bare feel of water,
woodman, to the wrinkled timber

When nesting starts I move out. Leaving the thickety places for the
birds. Redstart, Pied Flycatchers. Or if I'm thinning, say every twelve
trees I'll orange-tape what I want to keep. I'll find a fine one, a maiden
oak, well-formed with a good crop of acorns and knock down the
trees around it. And that tree'll stand getting slowly thicker and taller,
taking care of its surroundings, full of birds and moss and cavities
where bats'll roost and fly out when you work into dusk

woodman working into twilight
you should see me in the moonlight
comb my cataract of hair,
at work all night on my desire

oh I could sing a song of Hylas,
how the water wooed him senseless,
I could sing the welded kiss
continuous of Salmacis

and bring an otter from your bowels
to slip in secret through my veils
to all the plump and bony pools
the dips the paps the folds the holes

Trees like that, when they fall the whole place feels different, differ-
ent air, different creatures entering the gap. I saw two roe deer wan-
dering though this morning. And then the wind's got its foot in and
singles out the weaklings, drawn up old coppice stems that've got no

branches to give them balance. I generally leave the deadwood lying.
They say all rivers were once fallen trees. Or tush it to one of the
paths, stacks of it with bracket fungus and it goes for pulp or pallets
or half-cleave it into fence-stakes

woodman working on the crags
alone among increasing twigs
notice this, next time you pause
to drink a flask and file the saws

the Combestone and the Broadstone
standing in sunbeam gown,
the O Brook and the Rowbrook
starlit everywhere you look

such deep woods it feels like indoors and then you look down
and see it's raining on the river

O Rex Nemorensis   the King of the
Oaks whose arms   Oakwoods who had
are whole trees   to be sacrificed to a
                                    goddess.

in spring when   'Dart Dart
the river gives   Every year thou
up her dead   Claimest a heart.'

I saw you
rise dragging your
shadows in water

all summer I
saw you soaked
through and sinking

and the crack
and shriek as
you lost bones

God how I
wish I could
bury death deep

under the river
like that canoeist
just testing his

near Newbridge, a
canoeist drowned

strokes in the
quick moving water
which buried him

O Flumen Dialis
let him be
the magical flame

River of Zeus, the god
of the Oak. In ancient
times the Flamen
Dialis was the priest
of Zeus

come spring that
lights one oak
off the next

and the fields
and workers bursting
into light amen

canoeist

On Tuesdays we come out of the river at twilight, wet, shouting, with
canoes on our heads.

the river at ease, the river at night.

We can't hear except the booming of our thinking in the cockpit hol-
low and the river's been so beautiful we can't concentrate.

they walk strong in wetsuits,
their faces shine,
their well-being wants to burst out

In the water it's another matter, we're just shells and arms, keeping ourselves in a fluid relation with the danger.

pond-skaters, water-beetles,
neoprene spray-decks
many-coloured helmets,

But what I love is midweek between Dartmeet and Newbridge; kayaking down some inaccessible section between rocks and oaks in a valley gorge which walkers can't get at. You're utterly alone, abandoning everything at every instant, yourself in continuous transition twisting down a steep gradient: big bony boulders, water squeezing in between them. Sumps and boils and stopper waves. Times when the river goes over a rock, it speeds up, it slaps into the slower water ahead of it and backs up on itself, literally curls over and you get white water sometimes as high as a bus or a house. Like last November, the river rose three or four foot in two hours, right into the fields and I drove like mad to get to Newbridge. I could hear this roaring like some horrible revolving cylinder, I was getting into the river, I hadn't warmed up, it was still raining, and the surface looked mad, touchy, ready to slide over, and there was this fence underwater, a wave whacked me into it

come falleth in my push-you where it hurts
and let me rough you under, be a laugh
and breathe me please in whole inhale

come warmeth, I can outcanoevre you
into the smallest small where it moils up
and masses under the sloosh gates, put your head,

it looks a good one, full of kiss
and known to those you love, come roll it on my stones,
come tongue-in-skull, come drinketh, come sleepeth

I was pinioned by the pressure, the whole river-power of Dartmoor, not even five men pulling on a rope could shift me. It was one of those

experiences—I was sideways, leaning upstream, a tattered shape in a
perilous relationship with time

will you rustle quietly and listen to what I have to say now
describing the wetbacks of stones golden-mouthed and
making no headway, will you unsilt

how water orders itself like a pack of geese goes up
first in tatters then in shreds then in threads
and shucking its pools crawls into this slate and thin limestone phase

three hayfields above Buckfast where annual meadow grasshoppers
flower and fly to the tune of ribbed stalks rubbed.
will you swim down and attend to this foundry for sounds

this jabber of pidgin-river
drilling these rhythmic cells and trails of scales,
will you translate for me blunt blink glint.

is it span of eyes trammeling under the rain-making oaks
among stones the colour of magpies is it
suddenly though a padlocked gate

a green lane sliptoes secretly to the unseen
steep woods and cows the far side and
town boys sneak here after school: 'once   town boys

I jumped off the bus, I walked straight across, it was ice
now this is the real river, this is the Queen of the Dart
where it jinks down like through lawns almost'

the way I talk in my many-headed turbulence
among these modulations, this nimbus of words kept in motion
sing-calling something definitely human,

will somebody sing this riffle perfectly as the invisible river
sings it, quite different from this harsh primary
repertoire of murmurs, without any hardware

of stones and jointed sticks, one note
that rives apart the two worlds without any crossing
'I could show you a place it shallows over rocks

where the salmon flip out sometimes right onto the stones or they
        used to
and you could catch them bare-handed, now listen to this,
I was lugging this fish the size of myself,

taking the short-cut through the Abbey and up,
picture it, up comes a monk and imagine
he gives me a suitcase to smuggle it out past the bailiff . . .'

Smuggle it under the threshold of listening
into the ark of the soul, where the invisible
clear first water, the real Dart

writhes like a black fire, smelling of fish and soil
and traces a red leaf flood mark
and catches a drift of placer gold in her cracks

tin-extractor

you can go down with a wide bowl, where it eddies round bends or
large boulders. A special not easy motion, you fill it with gravel and a
fair amount of water, you shake it and settle it and tilt it forward. You
get a bit of gold, enough over the years to make a wedding ring but
mostly these dense black stones what are they?

He puts them in Hydrochloric acid, it makes his fingers yellow, but
they came up shiny, little wobbly nuts of tin

when I realised what I was onto in my own fields, I began to work
slowly upriver looking for shodes, the bigger tin-stones that lie close

to the source. I followed it up a brook of the Dart and built my own
alluvial plant with a pump re-circulating the water and a bucket on a
drag-line bopping it out and bingo

Glico of the Running Streams   named varieties of
and Spio of the Boulders-Encaved-In-The-River's-Edges   water

and all other named varieties of Water
such as Loops and Swirls in their specific dialects
clucking and clapping

Cymene and Semaia, sweeping a plectrum along the stones
and the stones' hollows hooting back at them
off-beat, as if luck should play the flute

can you hear them at all,
         muted and plucked,
muttering something that can only be expressed as
hitting a series of small bells just under the level of your
   listening?

you rinse it through a shaking screen, you take out a ton of gravelly
mud for say fifty pounds of tin and then you smelt it, 1,300 degrees C,
that's amazingly hot, that's when steel begins to burn and just as it
turns it starts melting, evaporating, half your tin disappearing into
the air

can you hear them rustling close by,
passing from hand to hand
a little trail of tin more than the weight of stone
and making the swish of swinging and regaining
   equilibrium?

Syrinx and Ligea groping through low-lit stalls
with silt in their mouths,
can you not hear them at all? not even the Rain

starting in several places at once
or a Fly's Foot typing on water?

not even the Stockdove-Falling-
Upwards-Through-Inverted-Trees

and calling prrrrooo prrrooo, who's
stirring the water about, who's up
the green end of the river dislodging stones?

I, Pol de Zinc, descended from the Norman, keeper of the coin, entre-
preneur, allrounder and tin extractor the last of a long line

William Withycombe, Alex Shawe, John Dawe,
    William Friend

and I. Keeper of the Woollen Mills, a fully vertical
    operation,
adding a certain amount of detergent, non-ionic,
    reasonably biodegradable,
which you have to, when you see how the wool comes in,
greasy with blue paint, shitty and sweaty with droppings
    dangling off it.

worker at Buckfast
Woollen Mills

Unfortunately sheep don't use loopaper.

it's all very well the fishermen complaining
but I see us like cormorants, living off the river.
we depend on it for its soft water
because it runs over granite and it's relatively free of
    calcium
whereas fishermen for what for leisure

the Woollen Mill has a
license to extract river
water for washing the
wool and for making
up the dyes

tufting felting hanks tops spindles slubbings
hoppers and rollers and slatted belts
bales of carded wool the colour of limestone
and wool puffs flying through tubes distributed by cyclones

wool in the back of the throat, wool on ledges,
in fields and spinning at 5,000 rotations per minute—
and look how quickly a worker can mend an end
what tentacular fingers moving like a spider,
splicing it invisibly neat look what fingers could be—

cotton warp, jute weft, wool pile, they work
lip-reading in a knocking throbbing bobbining hubbub
transporting the web on slatted belts with a twist to get it
    transverse,
then out for lunchbreak, hearing the small sounds of the day

That smell of old wet sheep.
I can stand by the fleece pile and pick out the different breeds:
this coarse lustrous curly one from Dartmoor,
this straighter one's a blackface from Scotland.

We pull apart the fleeces and blend them, we get a mountain, a tor of
wool, and load it onto hoppers for washing and keep combing it out,
because the lie of wool isn't smooth and cylindrical like human hair,
it's scaly like a fish or pine cone, which is why you get felting when
the scales get locked and can't release.

We do pure wool, one of the last places—red carpets, for Japanese
weddings. Which we dye in pressure vessels, 600 different shades, it's
skilled work, a machine with criss-cross motion makes up the hanks
and we hang them in the dye-house. Bear in mind if it rains, there's
peat in the river-water, full of metals, tin and such-like which when
you consider dyes are mostly metals, we split the web and rub it into
slubbings and from there onto bobbins. We stretch and wind it on a
spinning frame—a ring and travel arrangement twists it in the op-
posite direction and we end up with two-ply, a balanced twist, like
the river

Theodore Schwenke

'whenever currents of water meet the confluence is
    always the place

where rhythmical and spiralling movements may arise,
spiralling surfaces which glide past one another in
    manifold winding and curving forms
new water keeps flowing through each single strand of water
whole surfaces interweaving spatially and flowing past each other
in surface tension, through which water strives to attain
    a spherical drop-form'

wound onto reels and packed into bales
tied with polypropylene and cling film to keep it dry on
    the sea.

all day my voice is being washed away
out of a lapse in my throat

at Staverton Ford,
John Edmunds being
washed away, 1840

like after rain
little trails of soil-creep
loosen into streams

if I shout out,
if I shout in,
I am only as wide
as a word's aperture

but listen! if you listen
I will move you a few known sounds
in a constant irregular pattern:
flocks of foxgloves spectating slightly bending . . .

o I wish I was slammicking home
in wet clothes, shrammed with cold and bivvering but

this is my voice
under the spickety leaves,
under the knee-nappered trees
rustling in its cubby-holes

and rolling me round, like a container
upturned and sounded through

and the silence pouring into what's left maybe eighty
  seconds

                                                          silence

Menyahari—we scream in mid-air.
We jump from a tree into a pool, we change ourselves
into the fish dimension. Everybody swims here
under Still Pool Copse, on a saturday,
slapping the water with bare hands, it's fine once you're
    in.

Is it cold? Is it sharp?

I stood looking down through beech trees.
When I threw a stone I could count five before the
    splash.

Then I jumped in a rush of gold to the head,
through black and cold, red and cold, brown and warm,
giving water the weight and size of myself in order to
    imagine it,
water with my bones, water with my mouth and my
    understanding
when my body was in some way a wave to swim in,
one continuous fin from head to tail
I steered through rapids like a canoe,
digging my hands in, keeping just ahead of the pace of
    the river,
thinking God I'm going fast enough already, what am I,
spelling the shapes of the letters with legs and arms?

    S SSS   W

        Slooshing the Water open and

MMM

for it Meeting shut behind me

He dives, he shuts himself in a deep soft-bottomed
     silence
which underwater is all nectarine, nacreous. He lifts
the lid and shuts and lifts the lid and shuts and the sky
jumps in and out of the world he loafs in.
Far off and orange in the glow of it he drifts
all down the Deer Park, into the dished and dangerous
     stones of old walls
before the weirs were built, when the sea
came wallowing wide right over these floodfed
     buttercups.

Who's this beside him? Twenty knights at arms
capsized in full metal getting over the creeks;
they sank like coins with the heads on them still
     conscious
between water and steel trying to prize a little niche, a
hesitation, a hiding-place, a breath, helplessly
loosening straps with fingers metalled up, and the river
already counting them into her bag, taking her tythe,   'Dart Dart wants a
who now swim light as decayed spiderweb leaves.   heart'

Poor Kathy Pellam and the scout from Deadman's
     pool
tangled in the river's wires. There they lie
like scratchmarks in a stack of glass,
trapped under panes while he slides by
through Folly Pool through Folly Stickle,
hundreds of people hot from town with snorkels
dinghies minnow jars briefs bikinis
all slowly methodically swimming rid of their jobs.

Now the blessing, the readiness of Christ
be with all those who stare or fall into this river.
May the water buoy them up, may God grant them
extraordinary lifejacket lightness. And this child

watching two salmon glooming through Boathouse Pool
in water as high as heaven, spooked with yew trees
and spokes of wetrot branches—Christ be there
watching him watching, walking on this river.

water abstractor

and may He pull you out at Littlehempston, at the pumphouse, which
is my patch, the world's largest operational Sirofloc plant. Abstracting
water for the whole Torbay area. That and Venford and the Spine Main

(it's August and a
pendulum gladness swings just
missing our heads by
a millimetre the sun
unwrappers the hedgerows full
of sticky sweets and
sucks and each hour
the river alternates its
minnows through various cubes)

You don't know what goes into the water. Tiny particles of acids
and salts. Cryptospiridion smaller than a fleck of talcum powder
which squashes and elongates and bursts in the warmth of the
gut. Everything is measured twice and we have stand-bys and
shut-offs. This is what keeps you and me alive, this is the real work
of the river.

This is the thirst that draws the soul, beginning
at these three boreholes and radial collectors.
Whatever pumps and gravitates and gathers
in town reservoirs secretly can you follow it rushing
under manholes in the straggle of the streets
being gridded and channelled up
even as he taps his screwdriver on a copper pipe
and fills a glass. That this is the thirst that streaks
his throat and chips away at his bones between lifting
the glass and contact whatever sands the tongue,
this draws his eyehole to this space among

two thirds weight water and still swallowing.
That now and then it puts him in a stare
going over the tree-lit river in his car

Jan Coo! Jan Coo!
have you any idea what goes into the water?

I have verified the calibration records

have you monitored for colour and turbidity?

I'm continually sending light signals through it, my
    parameters are back to back

was it offish? did you increase the magnetite?

180 tonnes of it. I have bound the debris and skimmed
    the supernatant

have you in so doing dealt with the black inert matter?

in my own way. I have removed the finest particles

did you shut down all inlets?

I added extra chlorine

have you countervailed against decay?
have you created for us a feeling of relative invulnerability?

I do my best. I walk under the rapid gravity filters, under the clarifier
with the weight of all the water for the Torbay area going over me, it's
a lot for one man to carry on his shoulders.

wave the car on, let him pass, he has
sufficiently conducted himself under the pressure of
    self-repetition,

tomorrow it continues with the dripdripdripdrip of samples,
polyelectrolite and settlementation and twizzling scum and.

Exhausted almost to a sitstill,
letting the watergnats gather, for I am no longer   the river meets the
Sea at the foot of
Totnes Weir
able to walk except on a slope,

I inch into the weir's workplace,
pace volume light dayshift nightshift
water being spooled over, now

my head is about to slide—furl up my eyes,
give in to the crash of
surrendering riverflesh falling, I

come to in the sea I dream
at the foot of the weir, out here asleep
when the level fills and fills and covers the footpath,

the stones go down, the little mounds of sand
and sticks go down, the slatted walkway
sways in flood, canoes glide among trees,

trees wade, bangles of brash on branches,
it fills, it rains, the moon
spreads out floating above its sediment,

and a child secretly sleepwalks
under the frisky sound of the current
out all night, closed in an egg of water

(Sleep was at work and from the mind the mist   a dreamer
spread up like litmus to the moon, the rain
hung glittering in mid-air when I came down
and found a little patch of broken schist
under the water's trembling haste.

It was so bright, I picked myself a slate
as flat as a round pool and threw my whole
thrust into it, as if to skim my soul.
and nothing lies as straight as that stone's route
over the water's wobbling light;
it sank like a feather falls, not quite
in full possession of its weight.

I saw a sheet of seagulls suddenly
flap and lift with a loud clap and up
into the pain of flying, cry and croup
and crowd the light as if in rivalry
to peck the moon-bone empty
then fall all anyhow with arms spread out
and feet stretched forwards to the earth again.
They stood there like a flock of sleeping men
with heads tucked in, surrendering to the night.
whose forms from shoulder height
sank like a feather falls, not quite
in full possession of their weight.

There one dreamed bare clothed only in his wings
and one slept floating on his own reflection
whose outline was a point without extension.
At his wits' end to find the flickerings
of his few names and bones and things,
someone stood shouting inarticulate
descriptions of a shape that came and went
all night under the soft malevolent
rotating rain. and woke twice in a state
of ecstasy to hear his shout
sink like a feather falls, not quite
in full possession of its weight.

Tillworkers, thieves and housewives, all enshrined
in sleep, unable to look round; night vagrants,
prisoners on dream-bail, children without parents,

free-trading, changing, disembodied, blind
dreamers of every kind;
even corpses, creeping disconsolate
with tiny mouths, not knowing, still in tears,
still in their own small separate atmospheres,
rubbing the mould from their wet hands and feet
and lovers in mid-flight
all sank like a feather falls, not quite
in full possession of their weight.

And then I saw the river's dream-self walk
down to the ringmesh netting by the bridge
to feel the edge of shingle brush the edge
of sleep and float a world up like a cork
out of its body's liquid dark.
Like in a waterfall one small twig caught
catches a stick, a straw, a sack, a mesh
of leaves, a fragile wickerwork of floodbrash,
I saw all things catch and reticulate
into this dreaming of the Dart
that sinks like a feather falls, not quite
in full possession of its weight)

I wake wide in a swim of
seagulls, scavengers, monomaniac, mad
rubbish pickers, mating blatantly, screaming

and slouch off scumming and flashing and hatching flies
to the milk factory, staring at routine things:

dairy worker (river
water was originally
used to cool the milk)

looking down the glass lines: bottles on belts going round bends.
Watching out for breakages, working nights. Building up prestige. Me
with my hands under the tap, with my brain coated in a thin film of
milk. In the fridge, in the warehouse, wearing ear-protectors.

I'm in a rationalised set-up, a superplant. Everything's stainless and
risk can be spun off by centrifugal motion: blood, excrement, faecal
matter from the farms

have you forgotten the force that orders the world's fields
and sets all cities in their sites, this nomad
pulling the sun and moon, placeless in all places,
born with her stones, with her circular bird-voice,
carrying everywhere her quarters?

I'm in milk, 600,000,000 gallons a week.

processing, separating, blending. Very precise quantities of raw milk
added to skim, piped into silos, little screwed outlets pouring out
milk to be sampled. Milk clarified milk homogenised and pasteurised
and when it rains, the river comes under the ringmesh netting, full of
non-potable water. All those pathogens and spoilage organisms! We
have to think of our customers. We take pride in safety, we discard
thirty bottles either side of a breakage. We've got weights and checks
and trading standards

and a duck's nest in the leat with four blue eggs

and all the latest equipment, all stainless steel so immaculate you can
see your soul in it, in a hairnet, in white overalls and safety shoes.

sewage worker

It's a rush, a sploosh of sewage, twenty thousand cubic metres being
pumped in, stirred and settled out and wasted off, looped back, mac-
erated, digested, clarified and returned to the river. I'm used to the
idea. I fork the screenings out—a stink-mass of loopaper and what-
haveyou, rags cottonbuds, you name it. I measure the intake through
a flume and if there's too much, I waste it off down the stormflow, it's
not my problem.

When you think of all the milk we get from Unigate, fats and proteins
and detergents foaming up and the rain and all the public sewers
pumping in all day, it's like a prisoner up to his neck in water in a cell
with only a hand-pump to keep himself conscious, the whole place is
always on the point of going under.

So we only treat the primary flow, we keep it moving up these screws, we get the solids settled out and then push the activated sludge back through. Not much I can do.

I walk on metal grilles above smelly water, I climb the ladder, I stand on a bridge above a brown lagoon, little flocs of sludge and clarified liquor spilling over the edge of the outer circle. The bridge is turning very slowly, sweeping the spill-off round and I'm thinking illicit sneaking thoughts—no one can see me up here, just me and machinery and tiny organisms.

I'm in charge as far as Dartmoor, the metabolism of the whole South West, starting with clouds and flushing down through buildings and bodies into this underground grid of pipes, all ending up with me up here on my bridge—a flare of methane burning off blue at one end of the works and a culvert of clean water discharging out the other end, twenty BOD, nine ammonia, all the time, as and when

It happened when oak trees were men
when water was still water.
There was a man, Trojan born,
a footpad, a fighter:

Brutus, grandson of Aeneas.
But he killed his parents.
He shut his heart and sailed away
with a gang of exiled Trojans;

a hundred down and outs the sea
uninterestedly threw
from one hand to the other, where
to wash this numbness to?

An island of undisturbed woods,
rises in the waves,
a great spire of birdsong
out of a nave of leaves.

There a goddess calls them,
'Take aim, take heart,
Trojans, you've got to sail
till the sea meets the Dart.

Where salmon swim with many a glittering
and herons flare and fold,
look for a race of freshwater
filling the sea with gold.

If you can dip your hand down
and take a fish first go
or lean out and pick and oyster
while a seal stares at you,

then steer your ships into its pull
when the tide's on the rise
at full moon when the river
grazes the skirts of the trees

and row as far as Totnes
and there get out and stand,
outcasts of the earth, kings
of the green island England.'

Thirty days homeless on the sea,
twelve paces, then turn,
shacked in a lean-to ship,
windlash and sunburn.

Thirty days through a blue ring
suspended above nothing,
themselves and their flesh-troubled souls
in sleep, twisting and soothing.

They wake among landshapes,
the jut-ends of continents

foreign men with throats to slit;
a stray rock full of cormorants.

They sail into the grey-eyed rain,
a race of freshwater
fills the sea with flecks of peat,
sparrows shoal and scatter.

And when they dip their hands down
they can touch the salmon,
oysters on either side,
shelduck and heron.

So they steer into its pull
when the tide's on the rise,
at full moon when the river
grazes the skirts of the trees.

Silent round Dittisham bend,
each pause of the oar
they can hear the tiny sounds
of river crabs on the shore.

A fox at Stoke Gabriel,
a seal at Duncannon,
they sing round Sharpham bend
among the jumping salmon.

At Totnes, limping and swaying,
they set foot on the land.
There's a giant walking towards them,
a flat stone in each hand:

stonewaller

You get upriver stones and downriver stones. Beyond Totnes bridge
and above Longmarsh the stones are horrible grey chunks, a waste
of haulage, but in the estuary they're slatey flat stones, much darker,
maybe it's to do with the river's changes. Every beach has its own

species, I can read them, volcanic, sedimentary, red sandstone, they all nest in the Dart, but it's the rock that settles in layers and then flakes and cracks that gives me my flat walling stone,

They estuary's my merchant. I go pretty much the length and breadth of it scrudging stuff for some tiny stretch of wall, looking for the fault lines and the scabs of crystals and the natural coigns which are right-angled stones for corners.

I'm struggling now to find the really lovely stones I dream of: maroon stones perfect ellipses—but it's not just stones, sometimes huge bits of wood with the texture of water still in them in the plane of movement, a kind of camber.

I've made barns, sheds, chicken houses, goose huts, whatever I require, just putting two and two together, having a boat and a bit of space that needs squaring; which is how everything goes with me, because you see I'm a gatherer, an amateur, a scavenger, a comber, my whole style's a stone wall, just wedging together what happens to be lying about at the time.

I love this concept of drift, meaning driven, deposited by a current of air or water. Like how I came by the boat, someone just phoned and said I've got this eighteen-foot crabber and one thing led to another. Here I am now with a clinker-built launch.

But it's off the river at the moment, it gets a lot of wear and tear going aground on hard rocks and carrying a tonnage of stone around. I haven't worked it for six months, hence my agitated state, I keep looking over my shoulder, I dream my skin's flaking off and silting up the house; because the boat's my aerial, my instrument, connects me into the texture of things, as I keep saying, the grain, the drift of water which I couldn't otherwise get a hold on.

A tree-line, a slip-lane, a sight-line, an eye-hole, whatever it is, when you're chugging past Sharpham on a fine evening, completely flat, the water just glows. You get this light different from anything on land, as if you're keeping a different space, you're in a more wobbly element like a wheelbarrow, you can feel the whole earth tipping, the hills shifting up and down, shedding stones as if everything's a kind of water

Oceanides Atlanta Proserpina Minerva   boat voices

yachts with their river-shaking engines

Lizzie of Lymington Doris of Dit'sum

bending the firey strands under their keels, sheathed in the flying fields and fleeing the burden of being

two sailing boats, like prayers towing their wooden tongues
Naini Tal, Nereid of Quarr

and the sailmaker grabbing his sandwich,
the rich man bouncing his powerboat like a gym shoe,

the boatyard manager, thriving in the narrow margin between storing boats and keeping them moving, costing and delegating, structuring deals and wrapping up proposals

the shipwright, the caulker, the coutersunk copper nail

there goes the afternoon, faster than the rowers breathe, they lever
    and spring
and a skiff flies through like a needle worked loose from its compass

under the arch where Mick luvs Trudi
and Jud's heart
has the arrow locked through it

six corn-blue dinghies banging together
Liberty Belle, Easily Led, Valentine, L'Amour, White Rose and Fanny

and there goes Westerly Corsair Golden Cloud and Moonfire
Windweaver Sunshadow Seawolf

in the shine of a coming storm when the kiosk is closed
and gulls line up and gawp on the little low wall

there goes a line of leaves, there goes winter there goes the river at the
speed of the woods coming into flower a little slower than the heron
a little slower than a make-do boat running to heel with only a few
galvanised bits and a baler between you and your watery soul

there goes spring, there goes the lad from Kevicks
sailing to New Zealand in a tiny catamaran to find his girlfriend,
a wave washes out his stove, he's eating pasta soaked in seawater
and by the time he gets there she's with someone else

Troll, Fluff, Rank, Bruckless,
Bootle Bumtrink, Fisher 25,
Tester, Pewter, Whistler, Smiler
Jezail, Saith Seren, Pianola, Windfola,
Nanuk, Callooh, Shereefah

it's taken twenty years,   boatbuilder
every bit of spare cash,
it started as a dream, I did some sketches,
I had to build myself a shed to make it in

Freeby
Moody
Loopy Lou

every roll of fibre glass two hundred quid, it has to be sandwiched
round foam and resined, the whole thing rubbed over with powdered
glass and sanded by hand, but you can make fantastic shapes: eigh-
teen drawers in the galley not one the same size, two rudders—you
could sell them to the Tate

Checkmate Knot Shore

now if this was a wooden boat you'd have to steam the planks, they
used to peg them on the tide line to get salt into the timber; you can
still see grown oak boats, where you cut the bilge beams straight out
of the trees, keeping the line sweet, fairing it by eye, it's a different
mindset—when I was a boy all boats leaked like a basket, if you were
sailing you were bailing

Merry Fiddler Music Maker Island Life Fiesta

but give us a couple more years we'll be out of here, in the Med, soak-
ing up the sun, lying on the netting watching dolphins, swapping
a boatnail for a fish, we'll be away from all these cars, all this rain,
that's what the dream is that's what this boat is—for twenty years
now our only way out's been building it

like a ship the shape of flight
or like the weight that keeps it upright
or like a skyline crossed by breath
or like the planking bent beneath
or like a glint or like a gust
or like the lofting of a mast

such am I who flits and flows
and seeks and serves and swiftly goes—
the ship sets sail, the weight is thrown,
the skyline shifts, the planks groan,
the glint glides, the gust shivers
the mast sways and so does water

then like a wave of the flesh of wind
or like the flow-veins on the sand
or like the inkling of a fish
or like the phases of a splash
or like an eye or like a bone
or like a sandflea on a stone

such am I who flits and flows
and seeks and serves and swiftly goes—
the wave slides in, the sand lifts,
the fish fades, the splash drifts,
the eye blinks, the bone shatters,
the sandflea jumps and so does water

Back in the days when I was handsome and the river   salmon netsman and
was just river—   .   poacher

not all these buoys everywhere that trip your net so that you've got to
cut the headrope and the mesh goes fshoo like a zip.
Terrifying.
And there was so many salmon you could sit up to your knees in dead
fish keeping your legs warm.
I used to hear the tramp tramp tramp under my window of men going
down to the boats at three in the morning.

Low water, dead calm.

You don't know what goes on down there.
You go to bed, you switch out the light.
There's three of us in the pub with our hands shaking:
Have a beer mate, you're going out . . .
We daren't say anything, they can guess what we're onto
because the adrenalin's up and we're
jumping about like sea trout eeeeeeeeee
I haven't calmed down since a week ago,
I was standing under a sheer wall
with a bailiff above me flashing his torch over the river.
I put my hand up and touched his boot
and it's making my hair fall out remembering it.
Drink up now. Last orders. Low water. Dead calm.

When the sun goes down the wind drops.
It's so quiet you could fall asleep at the paddles.
That's when you can hear them jumping—

slap slap—you've got to be onto it.
It had a dog once who could sense a salmon.

That's your legal fisherman, he's watching and listening,
he's got a seine net and he hauls out from the shore and
back in a curve, like this.
But more than likely he's got a legal right hand and a
rogue left hand and when he's out left-handed,
he just rows a mesh net straight across the river—a bloody wall.
In twenty minutes he's covered the cost of the net,
in an hour he's got a celebration coming.
That's where the crack is, that's when fishing pays.

Or if it's dawn or nightfall, the river's the weird colour
    of the sky,
you can see a voler as much as two miles away.
That's the unique clean line a salmon makes in water
and you make a speckle for which way he's heading.

Your ears are twitching for the bailiff,
the car engine, the rustle in the bushes.
Bam! Lights come on, you ditch the net—
stop running, x, we know who you are.

There's a scuffle. The skill's to time it right, to row out
    fast and shoot your net fast over the stern,
a risky operation when you're leaning out and the boat
    wobbles—
I saw a man fallover the edge once:
oo oo oooo . . .

Our boat went under between the wharf and steamer
    quay.
We'd got weights on board, more than you're meant to
and we were all three of us in the water. One drowned.
It's a long story, you've got to judge the tide

You've got to judge the tide precisely, you draw a
    semicircle back to land.
One man's up there pulling the net in, knuckles to
    ground, so the catch doesn't spill out under,
which is hard work till it gets to the little eddy offshore
    and then the river gathers it in for you.
You can see them in the bunt of the net torpedoing
    round.
Sometimes a salmon'll smack your arm a significant
    knock, so you'll pull it right up the mud.
Some people would perceive it dangerous, but we know
    what we're doing,
even when it's mud up to our thighs, we know the places
    where the dredger's taken the sand away
Foul black stuff, if you got out there you might well
    disappear
and people do die in this river.

Three men on an oystering expedition,
the tide flowing in, the wind coming down,
on a wide bit of the river.
They filled the boat too full, they all drowned.

Where are you going? Flat Owers.   oyster gatherers
Who's Owers? Ours.
A paddock of sand mid-river
two hours either side of low water.

Can I come over?
All kinds of weather
when the wind spins you round
in your fish-tin boat with its four-stroke engine.

Who lives here?
Who dies here?
Only oysters and often
the quartertone quavers of an oyster-catcher.

Keep awake, keep listening.
The tide comes in fast
and after a while it
looks like you're standing on the water

still turning and shaking your oyster bags.
Already the sea taste
wets and sways the world—what now?
Now back to the river.

Feel this rain.
The only light's
the lichen tinselling the trees.
And when it's gone, Flat Owers

is ours. We mouth our joy.
Oysters, out of sight of sound.
A million rippled
life-masks of the river.

I thought it was a corpse once when I had a seal in the
    net—huge—a sea lion.
They go right up to the weir.
They hang around by the catch waiting for a chance.

That's nothing—I almost caught a boat once.
On an S-bend. Not a sound.
Pitch dark, waiting for the net to fill, then
BOOM BOOM BOOM—a pleasure boat
with full disco comes flashing round the corner.
What you call a panic bullet—
ten seconds to get the net in,
two poachers pulling like mad
in slow motion strobe lights
and one man, pissed, leans over the side and says
helloooooooooooooo?

But if you're lucky, at the last knockings it's a salmon with his great hard bony nose—
you hit him with a napper and he goes on twitching in the boat asking for more, more to come, more salmon to come.
But there aren't many more these days. They get caught off Greenland in the monofilaments.
That's why we're cut-throats on weekdays.

We have been known to get a bit fisticuffs—
boats have been sunk, nets set fire.
Once I waited half an hour and
hey what's happening, some tosser's poaching the stretch below me,
so I leg it downriver and make a bailiff noise in the bushes

And if you find a poacher's net, you just get out your pocket knife and shred it like you were ripping his guts.

whose side are you on?
I've grown up on this river,
I look after this river,
what's your business?

beating the other boats to the best places:
sandy pools up Sharpham where the salmon holds back
    to rub the sea-lice off his belly.
He'll hold back waiting for the pressure of water
or maybe it's been raining and washed oil off the roads
    or nitrates and God knows what else
and he doesn't like his impressions up the weir.

Some days the river's dark black—that's the moor water.
But the dredger's got rid of those pools now. We tie up
    at Duncannon now.

We go there after work, we dash down a cup of tea and a sandwich,
then lie about chatting on the stones

and we're down the Checkers every Friday evening,
saying nothing, playing yooker,
in the bogs in twos and threes, sorting out the order of
    the River—
You're Mondays, you're everything down from Am,
my places is the blind spot under the bridge
and if anyone else turns up, break their legs

why is this jostling procession of waters,
its many strands overclambering one another,
so many word-marks, momentary traces
in wind-script of the world's voices,
why is it so bragging and surrendering,
love-making, spending, working and wandering,
so stooping to look, so unstopping,
so scraping and sharpening and smoothing and
    wrapping,
why is it so sedulously clattering
so like a man mechanically muttering
so sighing, so endlessly seeking
to hinge his fantasies to his speaking,
all these scrambled and screw-like currents
and knotty altercations of torrents,
why is this interweaving form as contiguously gliding
as two sisters, so entwined, so dividing,
so caught in this dialogue that keeps
washing into the cracks of their lips
and spinning in the small hollows
of their ears and egos
this huge vascular structure
why is this flickering water
with its blinks and side-long looks
with its language of oaks
and clicking of its slatey brooks
why is this river not ever
able to leave until it's over?

Dartmouth and Kingsweir—
two worlds, like two foxes in a wood,
and each one can hear the wind-fractured
closeness of the other.

I work the car ferry, nudge it over with a pilot boat,
backwards and forwards for twenty three years.

Always on the way over—to or fro—
and feeling inward for a certain sliding feeling
that loosens the solidity of the earth,
he makes himself a membrane through which everyone
    passes into elsewhere
like a breath flutters its ghost across glass.

I was working it the night the Penhilly lifeboat went down:
soaking, terrified, frozen—the last man out on the river.
But I never saw any ghosts. I came home drowning.
I walked into the house and there was my beautiful
    red-haired wife,
there wasn't a man over twenty-five that didn't fancy her.

I think of her in autumn, when the trees go this amazing colour round
    Old Mill Creek.
I go down there and switch off my engine.   Silence.
After a while you hear the little sounds of the ebb.
Or in winter, you can hear stalks of ice splintering under
    the boat.

Wholly taken up with the detail to hand,
he tunes his tiller, he rubs the winter between his fingers.

On a good day, I can hear the wagtails over the engine.
Or I'll hear this cough like a gentleman in the water,
I turn round and it's a seal.

Swift fragmentary happenings

that ferry him between where things are now
and why, disengaging his eyes from the question

naval cadet

twenty years old and I already know knots and lowering boats. I know
radar and sonar, I can cross the gym without touching the floor. I
can nearly handle a two-engine picket boat, turn it on a sixpence and
bring it alongside.

I'm officer-quality, I've been brutalised into courage. You could fire
me from a frigate and I'd be a high-kill sea-skimming weapon, I'd hit
the target standing to attention.

I've got serious equipment in my head: derricks and davits, sea-
pistols, fins and wings and noise signatures. When the Threat comes
I'll be up an hour before it with my boots bulled and my bed pulled
up. Then down the path to Sandquay and encounter it whatever it is.
I've got the gear and the capability.

Every morning I bang my head against the wall, I let it shatter and
slowly fill up with water. I'm prepared you see. I jog round the block,
I go like hell and there's the sea the whole of it measuring itself up
against my body, how strong am I? I can really run, I take two steps
at a time, I salute the painted Britannia.

I've got the knack of fear, I've done two acquaints in a dinghy, just
enough to get the feel of the wind, a hostile at the end of a rope. Would
I float? If the hull was damaged, how long can I hold my breath?

the day the ship went down and five
policemen made a circle round
the sand and something half imagined
was born in blankets up the beach

all that day a dog was running
backwards forwards, shaking the water's

feathers from its fur and down
the sea-front no one came for chips

and then the sun went out and almost
madly the Salvation Army's
two strong women raised and tapped
their softest tambourines and someone

stared at the sea between his shoes
and I who had the next door grave
undressed without a word and lay
in darkness thinking of the sea

I remember when I was a boy   remimberer
born not more than a mile from where I am now

a whole millennium going by in the form of a wave

Dad was pilot on the Dart
at two in the morning in a force nine gale
flashing a torch to lead her in
you can see the current sliding through that moment

over a thousand tons of ship plus cargo
the quay getting closer at full speed and at a certain pace

you get this pause superimposed on water I remember

two sisters, Mrs Allen and Mrs Fletcher
used to row the plums across from Dittisham
and one dawn there were seven crusader ships
in the same steady stream of wind

it isn't easy to make out
in driving rain through water when you consider
your eyes are made mostly of movement

the cod fleet and the coal hulks and the bunkers from the
    Tyne and
a man sitting straight-up, reading a book in the bows
    while his ship was sinking   (Humphrey Gilbert)

but that was way back, when a chap made his living from his wits,
when I still had my parting in the middle and you could pull up
forty thousand pilchards in one draft

I stood here, I saw a whole flock of water migrating,
I saw two square-rigged barges carrying
deals, battens, scantling, lathwood
going out again with empty casks,
bags of trickling particles, bones, salts

Lew Bird, Stormy Croker,   former pilots on the
tiny spasms of time cross-fixed into water   Dart

and that same night, Dad took a merchant ship out
and left her at Castle ledge and she was bombed
and I saw the flames for hours up over that hill there

                                     crabbers
two brothers, both sea-fishers. Left school at fifteen and joined the
supercrabbers, big boats working out of Dartmouth and when I say
working

Say it's stormy, you walk a thousand miles just to stand upright. Each
crab pot seventy pounds and the end ones that weigh the net down
about the weight of a washing machine, that's twenty tonnes of gear
per day and only five hours sleep. Plus it's high risk. We were out in a
hurricane twenty miles off the Scillies.

No greenery—when you're at sea it's all sea. Then you head for
Dartmouth and fifteen miles away you can smell the land, you smell
silage, you see lights and fires. You've got a thousand pounds for a
week's work, you've got five days to enjoy yourself. I went mad, I sent
my wife champagne in a taxi.

I taxi'd to Plymouth, gave the cabbie lunch and paid him to wait all day for me.

We got a reputation, smashing up the town a bit, what could we do? Age fifteen we were big money, it was like crabs were a free commodity, we could go on pulling them from the sea year after year, it was like a trap for cash. Not to mention what some crabbers pull up, they don't always set their pots where the crabs are.

Ten years of that you pay for it with your body. Arthritis in the thumbs, elbows, knees, shoulders, back. A friend of ours died twice lifting pots, literally died, he had two heart attacks and got up again.

So now we're rod-and-lining off small piss-pot boats and setting nets for whatever. Some days we don't catch anything. Don't catch don't eat. Me and my dog went six days without food last winter.

But we're fishermen, Matt, we won't starve
                              Sid, we're allergic
                                    to fish

But tell me another job where you can see the whole sunrise every morning. No clocking in, no time bell. In summer you can dive in, see whales jumping, catch turtles the size of a dory. You slap your hands on the boatside and tell me another job where a dolphin spooks you, looks you straight in the eye and lets you touch him. You don't know what you are till you've seen that

they start the boat, they climb
as if over the river's vertebrae
out of its body into the wings of the sea
rounding the Mew Stone, the last bone of the Dart
where the shag stands criticising the weather
and rolls of seals haul out and scrabble away
and the seal-watcher on his wave-ski
shouts and waves and slowly paddles out of sight.

I steer my wave-ski into caves
horrible to enter alone
The fur, the hair, the fingernails, the bones.

Flick out the torch, the only thread between down here and daylight
and count five while the sea suckles and settles.
Self-maker, speaking its meaning over mine.

At low water
I swim up a dog-leg bend into the cliff,
the tide slooshes me almost to the roof

and float inwards into the trembling sphere
of one freshwater drip drip drip
where my name disappears and the sea slides in to replace it.

There the musky fishy genital smell
of things not yet actual: shivering impulses, shadows, propensities,
little amorous movements, quicksilver strainings and restrainings:

each winter they gather here,
twenty seals in this room behind the sea, all swaddled
and tucked in fat, like the soul in its cylinder of flesh.

With their grandmother mouths, with their dog-soft eyes, asking
who's this moving in the dark? Me.
This is me, anonymous, water's soliloquy,

all names, all voices, Slip-Shape, this is Proteus,
whoever that is, the shepherd of the seals,
driving my many selves from cave to cave . . .

FROM

Woods etc.

✦ ✦

Sea Poem

what is water in the eyes of water
loose inquisitive fragile anxious
a wave, a winged form
splitting up into sharp glances

what is the sound of water
after the rain stops you can hear the sea
washing rid of the world's increasing complexity,
making it perfect again out of perfect sand

oscillation endlessly shaken
into an entirely new structure
what is the depth of water
from which time has been rooted out

the depth is the strength of water
it can break glass or sink steel
treading drowners inwards down
what does it taste of

water deep in its own world
steep shafts warm streams
coal salt cod weed
dispersed outflows and flytipping

and the sun and its reflexion
throwing two shadows
what is the beauty of water
sky is its beauty

Seabird's Blessing

We are crowds of seabirds,
makers of many angles,
workers that unpick a web
of the air's threads and tangles.

Pray for us when we fight
the wind one to one;
let not that shuddering strength
smash the cross of the wing-bone.

O God the featherer,
lift us if we fall;
preserve the frenzy in our mouths,
the yellow star in the eyeball.

Christ, make smooth the way
of a creature like a spirit
up from its perverse body
without weight or limit.

Holy ghost of heaven,
blow us clear of the world,
give us the utmost of the air
to heave on and to hold.

Pray for us this weird
bare place—we are screaming
O sky count us not as nothing
O sea count us not as nothing

Owl

last night at the joint of dawn
an owl's call opened the darkness

miles away, more than a world beyond this room

and immediately, I was in the woods again,
poised, seeing my eyes seen,
hearing my listening heard

under a huge tree improvised by fear

dead brush falling then a star
straight through to God
founded and fixed the wood

then out, until it touched the town's lights,
an owl's elsewhere swelled and questioned

twice, like you might lean and strike
two matches in the wind

Woods etc.

footfall, which is a means so steady
and in small sections wanders through the mind
unnoticed, because it beats constantly,
sweeping together the loose tacks of sound

I remember walking once into increasing
woods, my hearing like a widening wound.
first your voice and then the rustling ceasing.
the last glow of rain dead in the ground

that my feet kept time with the sun's imaginary
changing position, hoping it would rise
suddenly from scattered parts of my body
into the upturned apses of my eyes.

no clearing in that quiet, no change at all.
in my throat the little mercury line
that regulates my speech began to fall
rapidly the endless length of my spine

Wood Not Yet Out

closed and containing everything, the land
leaning all round to block it from the wind,
a squirrel sprinting in startles and sees
sections of distance tilted through the trees
and where you jump the fence a flap of sacking
does for a stile, you walk through webs, the cracking
bushtwigs break their secrecies, the sun
vanishes up, instantly come and gone.
once in, you hardly notice as you move,
the wood keeps lifting up its hope, I love
to stand among the last trees listening down
to the releasing branches where I've been—
the rain, thinking I've gone, crackles the air
and calls by name the leaves that aren't yet there

Sisyphus

This man Sisyphus, he has to push
his dense unthinkable rock
through bogs woods crops glittering
optical rivers and hoof-sucked holes,
as high as starlight as low as granite,
and every inch of it he feels
the vertical stress of the sky
draw trees narrow, wear water round
and the lithe, cold-blooded grasses
weighted so down they have to hang their tips like cats' tails;
and it rains it blows but the mad delicate world
will not let will not let him out
and when he prays, he hears God passing with a
swish at this, a knock at that.

There is not a soft or feeling part,
the rock's heart is only another bone;
now he knows he will not get back home,
his whole outlook is a black rock;
like a foetus, undistractedly listening
to the clashing and whistling and tapping of another world,
he has to endure his object,
he has to oppose his patience to his perceptions . . .
and there is neither mouth
nor eye, there is not anything
so closed, so abstract as this rock
except innumerable other rocks
that lie down under the shady trees
or chafe slowly in the seas.

The secret is to walk evading nothing
through rain sleet darkness wind,
not to abandon the spirit of repetition:
there are the green and yellow trees, the dog,

the dark barrier of water,
there goes the thundercloud shaking its blue wolf's head;
and the real effort is to stare
unreconciled at how the same things are,
but he is half aware he is
lost or at any rate straining
out of the earth into a lifted sphere
(dust in his hair, a dark blood thread from his ear)
and jumps at shapes, like on a country road,
in heavy boots, heading uphill in silence.

Once his wide-armed shadow
came at him kicking,
his monkey counterpart pinioned to the rock;
the two grappled and the rock
stopped dead, pushed between them in suspension
and it was fear, quivering motion
holding them there, like in the centre of a flower
the small anxiety that sets it open
and for an hour, all he could think was
caught in a state of shadow—this persistent
breathing pushing sound, this fear of falling,
fear of lucidity, of flight, of something
bending towards him, but he pushed he pushed
until the sun sank and the shadow slunk away.

'I woke early when the grass was still a standing choir,
each green flower lifting a drop of water—
an hour of everything flashing out of darkness,
whole trees with their bones,
whole rivers with their kicks and throws,
there I walked lifting a drop of water;
I came to this cold field, the crowded
smoky-headed grasses singing of patience:

'Oh what does it matter?' they sang,
'longer and longer and all day
on one foot is the practice of grasses'
which raised in me a terrible cry of hope
and there I stood, waiting for the sun
to draw the water from my head . . .'

But Sisyphus is confused; he has to think
one pain at a time, like an insect
imprisoned in a drop of water;
he tries again, he distorts his body to the task
and a back-pain passes slowly
low down in the spine—a fine red thread
that winds his hands and feet in the struggle of movement;
and Sisyphus is a hump, Sisyphus is a stone
somewhere far away, feeling the sun
flitter to and fro with closed eyes,
unable to loiter, an unborn creature
seeking a womb, saying Sisyphus Sisyphus . . .
and he stares forward but there's nothing there
and backward but he can't perceive it.

Song of a Stone

there was a woman from the north
picked a stone up from the earth.
when the stone began to dream
it was a flower folded in

when the flower began to fruit
it was a circle full of light,
when the light began to break
it was a flood across a plain

when the plain began to stretch
the length scattered from the width
and then the width began to climb
it was a lark above a cliff

the lark singing for its life
was the muscle of a heart,
the heart flickering away
was an offthrow of the sea

and when the sea began to dance
it was the labyrinth of a conscience,
when the conscience pricked the heart
it was a man lost in thought

like milk that sours in the light,
like vapour twisting in the heat,
the thought was fugitive—a flare of gold—
it was an iris in a field

and when the man began to murmur
it was a question with no answer,
when the question changed its form
it was the same point driven home

it was a problem, a lamentation:
'What the buggery's going on?
This existence is an outrage!
Give me an arguer to shout with!'

and when the arguer appeared
it was an angel of the Lord,
and when the angel touched his chest,
it was his heartbeat being pushed

and when his heart began to break
it was the jarring of an earthquake
when the earth began to groan
they laid him in it six by one

dark bigger than his head,
pain swifter than his blood,
as good as gone, what could he do?
as deep as stone, what could he know?

Autobiography of a Stone

on this air-borne earth where the one thrust of things is endlessly upward,
I, Stone, fell into affliction,
worse than
the annealing of glass through the whole series of endurable pains

and worse.
and that was when I, Stone, became
this final measure
of drawing my whole body inward into my skull.

I became Excluded Stone, Stone-in-hiding.
who lies not peering out
in a fold of the winds and
hearing myself being shouted for   oh

if the wind were a voice I could contend with . . .
but I am moving only very slowly,
lasting out earth and
keeping my gift under darkness.

Walking Past a Rose This June Morning

is my heart a rose?   how unspeakable
is my heart a rose?   how unspeakable
is my heart folded to dismantle?   how unspeakable
is a rose folded in its nerves?   how unspeakable
is my heart secretly overhanging us?   pause
is there a new world   known only to breathing?
now inhale what I remember.   pause.   how unbreathable

this is my heart out.   how unspeakable
this is my risen skin.   how unthinkable
this is my tense touch-sensitive heart
this is its mass made springy by the rain
this loosening compression of hope.   how unworkable
is an invisible ray lighting up your lungs?   how invisible?
is it a weightless rapture?   pause.   how weightless?

now trace a breath-map in the air.   how invisible?
is a rose a turning cylinder of senses?   how unspeakable
is this the ghost of the heart, the actual
the inmost deceleration of its thought?   how unspeakable
is everything still speeding around us?   pause
is my heart the centre?   how unbearable
is the rain a halo?   how unbearable

Head of a Dandelion

This is the dandelion with its thousand faculties

like an old woman taken by the neck
and shaken to pieces.

This is the dust-flower flitting away.

This is the flower of amnesia.
It has opened its head to the wind,
all havoc and weakness,

as if a wooden man should stroll through fire . . .

In this unequal trial, one thing
controls the invisible violence of the air,

the other gets smashed and will not give in.

One thing flexes its tail causing widespread devastation,
it takes hold of the trees, it blows their failings out of them,
it throws in sideways, it flashes the river upriver;

the other thing gives up its skin and bones,
goes up in smoke, lets go of its ashes . . .

and this is the flower of no property,
this is the wind-bitten dandelion
worn away to its one recalcitrant element

like when Osiris
blows his scales and weighs the soul with a feather.

Field

Easternight, the mind's midwinter

I stood in the big field behind the house
at the centre of all visible darkness

a brick of earth, a block of sky,
there lay the world, wedged
between its premise and its conclusion

some star let go a small sound on a thread.

almost midnight—I could feel the earth's
soaking darkness squeeze and fill its darkness,
everything spinning into the spasm of midnight

and for a moment, this high field unhorizoned
hung upon nothing, barking for its owner

burial, widowed, moonless, seeping

docks, grasses, small windflowers, weepholes, wires

Solomon Grundy

Born on Monday and a tiny
world-containing grain of light
passed through each eye like heaven through a needle.

And on Tuesday
he screamed for a small ear in which to hide.

He rolled on Wednesday, rolled his whole body
full of immense salt spaces, slowly
from one horizon to the other.

And on Thursday, trembling, crippled,
broke beyond his given strength and crawled.

And on Friday he stood upright.

And on Saturday he tested a footstep
and the sky came down and alit on his shoulder
full of various languages in which one bird doesn't answer to another.

And on Sunday he dreamed he was flying
and his mind grew gold watching the moon
and he began to sing to the brink of speaking

Poem for Carrying a Baby Out of Hospital

like glass, concealed but not lost in light,
has structured into it a stress
that will burst out
suddenly in a shock of cracks, it's all
a matter of terror to hold right
what has a will to fall
and water for instance has the same weakness

the way the level ends of stockstill water break
at the touch of a raindrip, it demands
that kind of calm to walk
with a wafer of glass which if you slip could sheer
straight through a foot or neck
o infinite fear
entirely occupied upon two hands

and even a cobalt blue ingot of glass,
if you think of it, purpose-built
to be melted away, its mass
has an effect which makes it light
it moves through light to the heart of emptiness
though a slight
tap on its surface opens its integral fault

Five Fables of a Length of Flesh

Man

I was once a man. Very tired.
Very gone-inwards glaring outwards at the road.
His pusky eyes, his threadbare hair,
feet frozen in his boots, back sore.

A mouldering man, a powdered and reconstituted one
walking the same so on and so on.
Rutty road. Winter etc.
Poached fields, all zugs and water.

I was dying to ditch his head,
maybe put his socks on a twig and stop
caring, just lie there staring up.
I would sing then I would sing if I could

work the words out through this opening,
so done in I was from carrying everything
lungs bones hands belonging to this man
and superintending the rise and fall of breathing.

But as it was, all night he wouldn't let
death help him out or lift me off his wet
skin or sleep, but slowly crept
muttering to himself not yet not yet.

§ §

Ferret

I was next a woman
and what happens once will happen all over again,
flitting out through the wetleaf ditches,
chuckling and snuffling.

Not all woman, not unfurred,
if she could sleep she might wake,
creeping under the neighbours' windows, rustling
    and whistling,
what happens once will happen all over again.

One night she began, like a ferret
slips out from the two-chambered holt of the heart,
she began to emerge. More and more
definite delicate lithe inarticulate

into the arms of her lover when
what happens once will happen all over again.
A frog
hopped under her red-alert eyes: She pounced.

      ⸾ ⸾

Frog

Who's there? I am.
Where from? The wetlands of the womb.
First green, then lame,
going in and out of the swing door of the body.

Then secretive
lachrymal
vitreous
gelatinous.

I peeped out and saw myself
sitting like a stone in the rain
resting between forms.
This, I surmised,

with its throatful of grudges,
with its lumbar and glandular gripes, its guts,
its tissues and issues and sinews,
this is frog. For the moment.

This is when the sun
feels into my rubbery-soft-already-swumaway flesh
and finds me still
wedged in my inner dark.

So I croaked and carked,
clothed in leather in the bubbling breeding pools,
grieving being born and grown
and rotted down and born

§ §

till I became a large-headed ash-coloured man
with long slouching ears,
living all alone in his hairy homespun body,
shitting and itching and scratching and eating;

who heard the crickets at twilight
amorously soliciting their wives all of willow-wand
    slimness,
little hieroglyphs in the grasses,
lifting their pale triangular heads.

Always describing and then discarding their
    throwaway world
and then leaping and listening to the tiny slippage
between real and technical time, I heard them
persistently telephoning and glorying in their
    lightness

saying 'Singing is who we are in this place.
We are made of digital sounds, we are seeking
to be slightly more precise than is possible,
whizzing around, trying to unconceal things
    literally momentary.'

From that day, I resolved to eat nothing but dew.
And did so and died, despite
my own huge eyes
that stared at me from behind.

§ §

Sheep

Crashed over backwards buried under all the layers
    of my body,
in this condition of contradictions
when the earth calls back her employee
from its long and regular work of falling and
    sleeping,

I lay in my last self, stricken, like a sheep on its back.
When up comes the jackel-headed god, the guide
    who herds the dead
and sniffed and frisked and found me already half
    rotted
in a little pile of teeth and broken bone laths

And said he could spare me in exchange for three
    truths.
Then first, I said, I don't want to see you again.
Second, I want you to go blind.
Third, I wish you and your kind would come to
    some violent end.

And off he went,
chasing some other scent,
muttering to himself
not yet not yet . . .

Hymn to Iris

Quick-moving goddess of the rainbow
You whose being is only an afterglow of a passing-through

Put your hands
Put your heaven-taken shape down
On the ground. Now. Anywhere.

Like a bent-down bough of nothing
A bridge built out of the linked cells of thin air

And let there be instantly in its underlight—
At street corners, on swings, out of car windows—
A three-moment blessing for all bridges

May impossible rifts be often delicately crossed
By bridges of two thrown ropes or one dropped plank

May the unfixed forms of water be warily leaned over
On flexible high bridges, huge iron sketches of the mathematics of
    strain
And bridges of see-through stone, the living-space of drips and
    echoes

May two fields be bridged by a stile
And two hearts by the tilting footbridge of a glance

And may I often wake on the broken bridge of a word,
Like in the wind the trace of a web. Tethered to nothing

River

in the black gland of the earth
the tiny inkling of a river

put your ear to the river you hear trees
put your ear to the trees you hear the widening
numerical workings of the river

right down the length of Devon,
under a milky square of light that keeps quite still

the river slows down and goes on

with storm trash clustered on its branches
and paper unfolding underwater
and pairs of ducks swimming over bright grass among flooded
     willows

the earth's eye
looking through the earth's bones

carried the moon carries the sun but keeps nothing

Tree Ghosts

a ballad with footnotes
(in which each letter commemorates a cut-down tree)

with thanks to Bram and Mary Bartlett and Clifford Harris

This is a bAllad for Clifford Harris
Who saw the last red squirrel on this estate.
A man of four long rods that slot together
Bending and trembling under a considerable topweight.

There was Jimmy Miller and Jack James, Brilliant axemen,
Bob Penn, a queen's scout, up a tree like a monkey,
Stan Ivy on transport. John Fulcher admin.
And this is Clifford Harris, the Last Red Squirrel man.

Whyoo whyoo whyoo, that's him making crosscuts
With bowsaws and pitsaws, I don't know how many years;
Anyone can slice Down but it requires a bit of accuracy
To get it all to fall like so, oak trees especially.

Put Clifford Harris on a great big mother oak
With lEgs Flinging out and all sorts of bulges,
He could bring her down as neat as my arms
While a red squirrel nips in and watches.

Mind you he was employed to catch Greys,
Two shillings a tail. He got all sorts of Hatred
But when it's your work you've got to get on with it.
He had long squirrel rods for poking the dreys.

AlumInium things, they wouldn't go up straight,
Which was one of the hardest jobs for your arms;
And plus you've got to go out when it's wet
And the rain runs rivers up the sleeves of your Jacket.

Well this is a ballad about those times,
Almost always there, you don't taKe a lot of notice,
When the red was still at large in the woods,
So tame you could talk to him, says Clifford Harris.

He says the red was a gentle littLe thing
Who'd hop up with tail back looking down on you motionless,
Always very busy at providing for the winter,
Whereas your grey is shy and not nearly so clever.

So I ask you to picture hiM walking by earsight
Down the rides at North Woods, with his rods and lunchpack
Through blocks of chiffchaffs singing in the broadleaves
And the odd nuthatch in the fissures of conifers.

Next thing he knows, there's a terrific Noise.
Yes sometimes it does sound weird in a wood,
Sometimes it's like the wind's on all fours
Bleeding to death and you never say a word;

Certain places where there's nothing but nettles
And wonderful ash trees and a glimpse of a rOe deer,
If you stop rustling about you can hear
Whatever the wind says when there's no one there.

Well Clifford he Peers round and sees three greys
Attacking a red. The red's all panicky
And clicking at Clifford as if saying 'help me!'
It's as if that sQuirrel was one of his family.

But what could he do? You can't step in.
It's the same as trees. Once they start to go
It cReaks and cracks and nothing can stop them.
WhooSh! Gone! It's like holding snow.

It's like the fuTure's got a certain momentum,
It's like Tony Webster rolled down the log load,
One minute up, Unroping the stanchions,
Next minute crippled to the end of his days.

And that was the Very last red squirrel.
Since then it's been nothing but greys.
It's like the Woodlark it's like many a one
That you take for granted; neXt thing it's gone.

It's like sheering wood from the small end up,
You're turning the lathe and layer by laYer,
WhizzZ! Something you'd never think would happen.
The tree's ghost floats into the air!

FOOTNOTES

A is for Ash Trees
the loftiest letters in the wooden alphabet
B is for Beech Trees and Birch Trees
made of many streaming blooming intucking unfurling
C is for Copse and Corpse
as G is for both Grove and Grave
in which you sow a person
and he puts forth silvery threads into the air
and AIR is for the varying shapes
made by the cavities of the mouth and throat
so that the soul is squeezed and shaken into VOICE

　　　₹ ₹

D E F is the Deaf and Dumb and Finger language of the branches
L M N is thousands of leaf-like sounds
that shadow forth for a moment in the wake of wind
like a rock or stick inscribes its drift in the scrolls of a river
I, by far the most solitary and inward-looking letter,
I is for Speech Impediment

in which the timber's stutter doesn't interest the woodman
and Hyale Crocale Phiale Meliae—these are for Dryads and Hamadryads,
their bodies tushed to one side to be slatted and planked up
whereas J and K are for Joists and Krucks
made of a Woodnymph's Joints and Kracks

O is the outline of the OldWood
and S is the Still Growing Ghost of the OldWood
in which the waters recompose as the vapour-forms of twigs and anti-
    twigs, roots and un-roots
and P and Q are Songs of eQuivocal Perplexity
issuing from the throats of Oaks
and T is for the Shakes which is when Timber if you cut it Green
it splits in a hot summer
plus you've got V which is like the funny bone of a conifer
and if you Bang it you get pins and needles
not to mention W which is a Woodlark
which is what emerges when the Larches drop their Aitches

but R is for Rowan, the Quicken Tree,
which is even now breathlessly quickening into wings tails crests
threads flames flumes fans palms scarves robes tubes
and perpetually interchangeable billows following one after another
and U is for the Unreadable Alphabet of its Leaves
each one a single phase out of the sequence of movements in the flight of birds
and X and Z are for the criss-crossed Zones
of the living and the dead wood
in which Y is for Yew, which grows by graves
and is said to spread a root like a kind of windpipe
to the mouth of every corpse

Moon Hymn

I will give you one glimpse
a glimpse of the moon's grievance
whose appearance is all pocks and points
that look like frost-glints

I will wave my hand to her
in her first quarter
when the whole world is against her
shadowy exposure of her centre

o the moon loves to wander
I will go clockwise and stare
when she is huge when she is half elsewhere
half naked, in struggle with the air

and growing rounder and rounder
a pert peering creature
I love her sidling and awkward
when she's not quite circular

o criminal and ingrown
skinned animal o moon
carrying inside yourself your own
death's head, your dark one

why do you chop yourself away
piece by piece, to that final trace
of an outline of ice
on a cupful of space?

The mud-spattered recollections
of a woman who lived her life backwards

I'll tell you a tale: one morning one morning I lay
in my uncomfortable six-foot small grave,
I lay sulking about a somewhat too short-lit
life both fruitful and dutiful.

It was death it was death like an inbreath fully inhaled
in the grief of the world when at last
there began to emerge a way out, alas
the in-snowing silence made any description difficult.

No eyes no matches and yet mathematically speaking
I could still reach at a stretch a wispish whiteish
last seen outline any way up, which could well be my own
were it only a matter of re-folding.

So I creased I uncreased and the next thing I knew
I was pulled from the ground at the appointed hour
and rushed to the nearest morgue to set out yet again
from the bed to the floor to the door to the air.

And there was the car still there in its last known place
under the rain where I'd left it, my husband etc.
even myself, in retrospect I was still there
still driving back with the past all spread out already in front of me.

What a refreshing whiff with the windows open!
there were the dead leaves twitching and tacking back
to their roosts in the trees and all it required
was a certain minimum level of inattention.

I tell you, for many years from doorway to doorway
and in through a series of rooms I barley noticed

I was humming the same tune twice, I was seeing the same
three children racing towards me getting smaller and smaller.

This tale's like a rose, once opened it
cannot reclose, it continues: one morning
one terrible morning for maybe the hundredth time
they came to insert my third child back inside me.

It was death it was death: from head to foot
I heard myself crack with the effort, I leaned and cried
and a feeling fell on me with a dull clang
that I'd never see my darling daughter again.

Then both my sons, slowly at first
then faster and faster, their limbs retracted inwards
smaller and smaller till all that remained
was a little mound where I didn't quite meet in the middle.

Well either I was or was not either living or dead
in a windowless cubicle of the past, a mere
8.3 light minutes from the present moment when at last
my husband walked oh dear he walked me to church.

All in one brief winter's day, both
braced for confusion with much shy joy,
reversed our vows, unringed our hands
and slid them back in our pockets God knows why.

What then what then I'll tell you what then: one evening
there I stood in the matchbox world of childhood
and saw the stars fall straight through Jimmy's binoculars,
they looked so weird skewered to a fleeting instant.

Then again and again for maybe the hundredth time
they came to insert me feet first back into nothing
complete with all my missing hopes—next morning
there was that same old humming thrum still there.

That same old humming thrumming sound that is either
my tape re-winding again or maybe it's stars
passing through stars coming back to their last known places,
for as far as I know in the end both sounds are the same.

Various Portents

Various stars. Various kings.
Various sunsets, signs, cursory insights.
Many minute attentions, many knowledgeable watchers,
Much cold, much overbearing darkness.

Various long midwinter Glooms.
Various Solitary and Terrible Stars.
Many Frosty Nights, many previously Unseen Sky-flowers.
Many people setting out (some of them kings) all clutching at stars.

More than one North Star, more than one South Star.
Several billion elliptical galaxies, bubble nebulae, binary systems,
Various dust lanes, various routes through varying thicknesses of Dark,
Many tunnels into deep space, minds going back and forth.

Many visions, many digitally enhanced heavens,
All kinds of glistenings being gathered into telescopes:
Fireworks, gasworks, white-streaked works of Dusk,
Works of wonder and/or water, snowflakes, stars of frost . . .

Various dazed astronomers dilating their eyes,
Various astronauts setting out into laughterless earthlessness,
Various 5,000-year-old moon maps,
Various blindmen feeling across the heavens in braille.

Various gods making beautiful works in bronze,
Brooches, crowns, triangles, cups and chains,
And all sorts of drystone stars put together without mortar.
Many Wisemen remarking the irregular weather.

Many exile energies, many low-voiced followers,
Watches of wisp of various glowing spindles,
Soothsayers, hunters in the High Country of the Zodiac,
Seafarers tossing, tied to a star . . .

Various people coming home (some of them kings). Various headlights.
Two or three children standing or sitting on the low wall.
Various winds, the Sea Wind, the sound-laden Winds of Evening
Blowing the stars towards them, bringing snow.

Excursion to the Planet Mercury

certain evenings a little before the golden
foam of the horizon has properly hardened
you can see a tiny iron island
very close indeed to the sun.

all craters and mirrors, the uncanny country
of the planet Mercury—a mystery
without I without air,
without you without sound.

in that violently magic little place
the sky is racing along
like a blue wrapper flapped and let go
from a car window.

now hot now cold
the ground moves fast,
a few stones frisk about
looking for a foothold

but it shales it slides
the whole concept is only
loosely fastened
to a few weak tweaks of gravity.

o the weather is dreadful there:
thousand-year showers of dust
all dandruff and discarded shells
of creatures too swift to exist:

paupers beggars toughs
boys in dresses
who come alive and crumble
at the mercy of metamorphosis.

no nothing accumulates there
not even mist
nothing but glimmering beginnings
making ready to manifest.

as for the catastrophe
of nights on Mercury,
hiding in a rock-smashed hollow
at about two hundred degrees below zero

the feather-footed winds
take off their guises there,
they go in gym shoes
thieving and lifting

and their amazed expressions
have been soundproofed, nevertheless
they go on howling
for gladness sheer gladness

Sonnet

Spacecraft Voyager 1 has boldly gone
into Deep Silence carrying a gold-plated disc inscribed with whale-song
it has bleeped back a last infra-red fragment of language
and floated way way up over the jagged edge
of this almost endless bright and blowy enclosure of weather
to sink through a new texture as tenuous as the soft upward pressure of
    an elevator
and go on and on falling up steep flights of blackness with increasing
    swiftness
beyond the Crystalline Cloud of the Dead beyond Plato beyond Copernicus
O meticulous swivel cameras still registering events
among those homeless spaces gathering in that silence
that hasn't yet had time to speak   in that increasing sphere
of tiny runaway stars notched in the year
now you can look closely at massless light
that is said to travel freely but is probably in full flight

NEW POEMS

Dunt

a poem for a nearly dried up river

Very small and damaged and quite dry,
a Roman Waternymph made of bone
tries to summon a river out of limestone.

Very eroded faded,
her left arm missing and both legs from the knee down,
a Roman Waternymph made of bone
tries to summon a river out of limestone.

Exhausted, utterly worn down,
a Roman Waternymph made of bone,
being the last known speaker of her language,
she tries to summon a river out of limestone.

Little distant sound of dry grass. Try again.

A Roman Waternymph made of bone,
very endangered now,
in a largely unintelligible monotone,
she tries to summon a river out of limestone.

Little distant sound as of dry grass. Try again.

Exquisite bone figurine with upturned urn,
in her passionate self-esteem, she smiles, looking sideways.
She seemingly has no voice but a throat-clearing rustle
as of dry grass. Try again.

She tries leaning,
pouring pure outwardness out of a grey urn.

Little slithering sounds as of a rabbit man in full nightgear.
Who lies so low in the rickety willowherb
that a fox trots out of the woods
and over his back and away. Try again.

She tries leaning,
pouring pure outwardness out of a grey urn.
Little lapping sounds. Yes.
As of dry grass secretly drinking. Try again.

Little lapping sounds yes
as of dry grass secretly drinking. Try again.

Roman bone figurine,
year after year in a sealed glass case,
having lost the hearing of her surroundings,
she struggles to summon a river out of limestone.

Little shuffling sound as of approaching slippers.

Year after year in a sealed glass case
a Roman Waternymph made of bone,
she struggles to summon a river out of limestone.

Pause. Little shuffling sound as of a nearly dried up woman
not really moving through the fields,
having had the gleam taken out of her
to the point where she resembles twilight. Try again.

Little shuffling clicking.
She opens the door of the church.
Little distant sounds of shutaway singing. Try again.

Little whispering fidgeting of a shutaway congregation
wondering who to pray to.
Little patter of eyes closing. Try again.

Very small and damaged and quite dry,
a Roman Waternymph made of bone
she pleads she pleads a river out of limestone.

Little hobbling tripping of a nearly dried up river
not really moving through the fields,
having had the gleam taken out of it
to the point where it resembles twilight.
Little grumbling shivering last ditch attempt at a river
more nettles than water. Try again.

Very speechless, very broken old woman,
her left arm missing and both legs from the knee down,
she tries to summon a river out of limestone.

Little stoved in sucked thin
low-burning glint of stones
rough-sleeping and trembling and clinging to its rights.
Victim of Swindon
puddle midden
slum of overgreened footchurn and pats
whose crayfish are cheap toolkits
made of the mud stirred up when a stone's lifted.

It's a pitiable likeness of clear running
struggling to keep up with what's already gone:
the boat the wheel the sluice gate,
the two otters larricking along. Go on.

And they say oh they say
in the days of better rainfall
it would flood through five valleys,
there'd be cows and milking stools
washed over the garden walls
and when it froze, you could skate for five miles. Yes go on.

Little loose end shorthand unrepresented
beautiful disused route to the sea,
fish path with nearly no fish in.

In a tidal valley

flat stone sometimes lit sometimes not
one among many moodswung creatures
that have settled in this beautiful
Uncountry of an Estuary

swans pitching your wings
in the reedy layby of a vacancy
where the house of the sea
can be set up quickly and taken down in an hour

all you flooded and stranded weeds whose workplace
is both a barren mud-site and a speeded up garden
full of lake-offerings and slabs of light
which then unwills itself listen

all you crabs in the dark alleys of the wall
all you mudswarms ranging up and down
I notice you are very alert and worn out
skulking about and grabbing what you can

listen this is not the ordinary surface river
this is not river at all this is something
like a huge repeating mechanism
banging and banging the jetty

very hard to define, most close in kind
to the mighty angels of purgatory
who come solar-powered into darkness
using no other sails than their shining wings

yes this is the Moon this hurrying
muscular unsolid unstillness
this endless wavering in whose engine
I too am living

Mud

this evening those very thin fence posts
struggled up out of the mud again
and immediately the meal began, there was
that flutter of white napkins of waders hurrying in

there was that bent old egret
prodding and poising his knife and fork
and so many mucous mudglands
so much soft throat sucking at my feet

I thought be careful this is deep mud this is
pure mouth it has such lip muscles
such a suction of wet kisses
the slightest contact clingfilms your hands

there goes that dunlin up to her chin in
the simmering dish of mush and
all night that seeping feeding sound
of moistness digesting smallness

and then I creep-slid out over the grey weed,
and all those slimy foodpods burst under me
I thought I know whose tongue I'm
treading on and under whose closed eye

every stone every shell every sock
every bone will be crammed in.
to my unease the meal went on and on
there were those queues of reeds

dipping their straws in the dead
there was that sly tide swiftly refilling
I thought reallly I should have webbed feet
I should have white wings to walk here

Fragment of an Unfinished Morning

Old moon, very old. Gets up at night. No sleep.
Horizon and back. No joy. She's only half herself. Half cancer.
Fumbling around her room with a pain in one side.

Every night a little yellower, as if the milk in her veins had gone sour.
As if her head was the last frost-crippled leaf left hanging on her neckbone.

≋ ≋

Enter a man.
Shuffling.
No shoes.

He speaks pain in Polish.
I hear him bumping on the bedroom wall.
Thirteen stone, footswollen man, with a rusted spine.
And his wife, sleeping in broken English.
Very old sorrows, very old dried sorrows
rattling in her head. She snores,
feeling like a stranger in her body. I'm sorry.

Cough cough cough.

That's him in pyjamas. He shuffles about all night.
He paces, faces the window, coughs, paces.
I can hear him muttering
to a small bright-pale moon with turned away eyes.

Another thousand years,
it's tiring to be always growing old.
He keeps living his life backwards and forwards,
backwards and forwards, but it doesn't help.
Window and back. No joy.
No way out. Not a glimmer.

≋ ≋

No answer.

≷ ≷

Enter the sky.
Old Moon at her window.
White face unwashed.
Face fading out.

Enter hundreds of moths in black uniforms
working nightshift on shaky wings,
but they can't make dark fast enough,
the grass is already shivering into its clothes.

There are geese coming down for their prayers.

You can hear a cricket being lit:
three strikes on the side of a matchbox . . .

≷ ≷

Pause.

≷ ≷

Neither silence nor a voice,
but a faint light in which the sky has been left open
and the draught goes straight in through the moon.

She gets gooseflesh, flutterish,
weakening in the grip of the light:
It frightens the life out of her—
all that molten steel—it's like white hot water—
she has to press her face to her face
to keep from folding or falling over . . .

≷ ≷

Enter the Window.
All cobwebbed up.
As bad as both eyes.

Tins upon tins upon tins,
lined up for coolness on the sill:
peas in brine, beans in sauce, prunes in juice, beef in fat . . .

Old man joined by his wife.
She wears her quilted dressing gown.
She puts her hand on the dog
and her neck keeps swelling with a gentle cooing,
seeing the same things, but aside and at much less speed . . .

≷ ≷

Enter the Dawn.

≷ ≷

Exit slowly the Moon,
all but her white face-powder
like a smudge of kiss,
and then gone

≷ ≷

and I can see the sun—at first uncertain,
only speaking with her fingers,
then suddenly the whole sky
moving upstage to describe itself:

Another thousand years as always at this hour
enter day after day the Dawn.
She is not a human.
She is colder, quicker,
more like a ghost but less damaged.

Like a rapid glance through a room underwater
being lifted and gone.

Enter day after day the Dawn by a window.
She is not a human.
More like an endless repetition that wears you down,
like a deep breath
and in the same breath gone. But quicker.
Enter softly the Dawn with one song.
She is not a human.
She is vaguer.
More veiled and clouded.
Like an undeveloped photo coming to its senses.
And exit.

Enter day after day the Dawn on the wire of a cobweb.
Enter old man. Be seated please.
No shoes. Can't sleep. Listening.

Enter the Dawn with two songs.
She is not a human.

Enter softly the Dawn to a man.
She touches the lyre of her cobweb. Twang.
And the Gloom undarkens a little.
Then exits.

Enter the Dawn three times.
Enter again with music.
She is not a human.
More like an overpowering almost suffocating green
with a little rain. Enter again.
Same time or a little earlier each morning,

enter the Dawn with music to a man.
Be seated please. No shoes. Can't sleep. Listening.

Enter the Dawn to a man in a series of songs.
Mother of the winds what a voice!
What a slow slipping off of the wet coat of the night and then gone . . .

≋ ≋

Pause.

Enter the Daylight. Exit.
Enter the Twilight. Exit.
Enter the Dawn. Exit.

Enter several times the Twilight,
followed slavishly by the Night.

Exit Old Man.

Alice Oswald is the author of three collections of poetry published in Britain: *The Thing in the Gap-Stone Stile,* which won the 1996 Forward Prize for best first collection; *Dart,* which won the 2002 T.S. Eliot Prize; and *Woods etc.,* which received the Geoffrey Faber Memorial Prize. She lives in Devon and is married with three children.

This book was designed by Ann Sudmeier. It is set in Berkeley Oldstyle type by Prism Publishing Center, and manufactured by Bookmobile on acid-free, 100 percent postconsumer wastepaper.